CELTIC
MYSTICISM

CELTIC
MYSTICISM

Your Personal Guide
to Celtic and Druid
Tradition

TRACIE LONG

wellfleet
press

CONTENTS

INTRODUCTION

The mystical tales of the Celts have captivated the human imagination across geography and time. Even when they're not in the forefront of our minds, they make their way into our stories, traditions, holidays, and daily lives. While we may casually know what fairies are or who King Arthur of the Round Table was, most don't know the roots of these magical fables. *Celtic Mysticism* aims to lay a foundation of understanding as to who the Celts were, what their spirituality meant to them, and the ways in which they interpreted the world around them—all of which shape their fascinating, and sometimes haunting, lore and magic.

For most, when we hear the word "Celtic," we automatically think of the Irish. While the Irish were and still are essential to Celtic culture, the Celts in fact sprang from a wide geographical, cultural, and historical cornucopia of peoples. Some of the deepest influences on Celtic culture come from the Irish, yes, but also the Scots, the Welsh, the Italians, the Spanish, the English, the Romans, the Christians, the pagans, and the superstitious. Because of this, and the ancient nature of their mystic traditions, it has been difficult to definitively pin down exactly what these origins were and from where they came. Different regional Celts spoke differing languages, and it was not common for them to write down or record anything. Therefore, Celtic mysticism is largely based on oral traditions that may vary depending on which culture is relaying the myth.

This book aims to represent as much foundational knowledge as possible without singling out any specific group. However, Druids are a relatively universal mainstay, the connective thread between all Celtic cultures, and their practices and ideologies are the very basis for Celtic mystical studies. They were powerful figures, being not only wise sages but also healers, advisors, genealogists, historians, storytellers, teachers, spiritual leaders, and so much more.

Celtic culture relied heavily on oral tradition; there's no evidence that they wrote things down as far as history, genealogy, myths, and general way of life, so most of what we know has been passed down orally by the Druids through generations in the form of mythic allegories. Mythic tales of gods controlling the weather and the elements of earth reveal how they interpreted the natural world, goddess-focused tales show how they understood love and fertility, and stories such as the Children of Lir depict their close family ties, to name a few.

The Druids, however, did develop what was considered to be an enchanted script, based on trees and their magical properties, called the Ogham (pronounced och'um). These symbols were used for some writing, but most typically used in the realm of magical practice. Ogham characters were carved into Druid's tools, such as a wand or a cauldron, to enhance their already powerful magic. And, just like the ancient Celtic culture that they so diligently preserved, Druids have survived through modern times. The Ancient Order of Druids is the oldest Druid order that exists to this day, whose members are called Neo-Druids—a word for modern druids. The Order was established in 1781 by a man named Henry Hurle in London, England. This Order represents England, Scotland, Wales, and the Commonwealth Nations, and can now be found in America, too.

Today, the core values of Druid philosophy have changed very little since ancient times, focusing on brotherly love, compassion for all living things, environmentalism, and helping those in need, but with an updated application and interpretation to adjust to the unique demands of modern life. For example, they no longer practice human or animal sacrifice, as the Romans claimed the Celts and Druids did in ancient times. What we can speculate about these brutal practices potentially being practiced is that they were done only in times of great need, if they were actually done at all. Our knowledge on this is based off the writings of Julius Caesar who, around 53 BC, was their bitter rival and often conqueror. It can be argued that his perceptions were skewed based on lack of understanding of the cultures and his motive to conquer their territories. While much information about the Celts and Druids has been gleaned from these writings, we must keep them in context and only take from them what we can surmise as fact.

With this book you will learn about the history of a resilient and almost supernatural people and the ideology they turned to for a fruitful existence. You will become familiar with the Druids and the fascinating ways in which they harnessed the magic of the natural world, originally for tribal survival, and currently for spiritual fortification and the health of all sentient beings and our Earth. We will discuss oral traditions and who was responsible for passing these down, as well as relay a few of their stories to offer a glimpse into their magical world and offer an understanding of who they were. While it's evident that the basis of Celtic spirituality was magic and a firm belief in deities, they were eventually influenced by the Roman Christians. In turn, Celtic spiritualism influenced Christianity, as evidenced by ancient texts of the Gospels that are embellished with Celtic mystical symbolism. Even those opposed to their spirituality and practices couldn't deny their love for Celtic lore and symbolism.

This book is designed to share the fascinating history of the Celts so that you can more easily appreciate the depth of their mythology, legends, and magic, then teach you how to apply their principles to your own daily life. Peppered throughout each chapter are fact boxes that will charm and inform you, while spells, rituals, and exercises will help to cement your understanding of this mysterious culture and give you tools that you can integrate into your life and your own belief systems, should you choose. It should be said that the Druids strictly forbid anyone who has not undergone their training and ordination to perform their spells or rituals. The activities, rituals, spells, and recipes in this book are based on ancient Celtic magic that has survived through paganism and witchcraft since the dawn of magic itself, and my own experiences. Through this introductory book, explore what the ancient Celts ate, how they migrated and why, where they lived, and how they used their resources to survive, both physically and spiritually.

One of the most important concepts to understand is the Celtic territories. This knowledge is essential because the Celts often migrated according to weather patterns, resource availability, to avoid tribal conflicts, or to distance themselves from war and colonizing armies, such as the ancient Romans. It is because of their migratory patterns that it can be difficult to nail down exactly what regions the Celts are originally from, and this highly contributed to the lack of a unified writing alphabet, which to this day impacts our access to their history. At the end of this introduction, I have included a map of Celtic territories around 250 BC. I encourage you to refer to this map as you learn of their locations, territories, and battles for land rights through the later chapters.

Although the wisdom touched on in this book is ancient, it is my hope that it will guide you to a deeper understanding of the charisma of the Celtic people and give you the insight to apply it today. By simply being curious and picking up this book, you have already embodied the popular old Celtic proverb "the questioning person is halfway to being wise."

THE CELTIC TERRITORIES

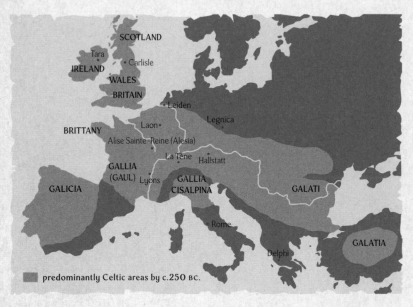

This map is a re-creation of the Celtic territories around the year 250 BC.

AN OLD IRISH BLESSING

May love and laughter light your days,
And warm your heart and home,
May good and faithful friends be yours,
Wherever you may roam.
May peace and plenty bless your world
With joy that long endures,
May all life's passing seasons,
Bring the best to you and yours.

CHAPTER 1

EARLY CELTIC LIFE

W hen thinking of who the Celts were, images of the Celtic cross and mysteriously robed Druids may be the first things that come to mind. While those identities do take root in Celtic lore, the Celts themselves consisted of a set of tribes that originated in central Europe who shared similar languages, religious beliefs, traditions, and ideologies. They have a long and tumultuous history of establishing territories, fighting off invaders, and instituting governmental monarchies. Chapter one aims to lay foundational knowledge of who the Celts were historically, where they lived, who they defended themselves against, and what the influences on their ancient beliefs were—all of which shape the modern Celtic identity, even despite a wide geographical reach and limited written record.

Throughout history, and stretching into modern times, the Celts have been regarded in relation to the Irish, Welsh, and Scottish peoples. Although the exact historical origins are unknown, it is widely agreed upon that the Celtic people originated during the Early Iron Age in western Europe, in around 600 BC. Gradually, they spread throughout Europe and across the sea into England, Wales, Scotland, and Ireland. Despite great distances between them, the Celtic tribes of Europe shared a similar outlook, belief system, language, and culture—which lives on in certain regions—and influenced foreign religions such as Christianity. The formidable Romans considered the Celts, and especially the Druids, to be a competing power during the Roman invasion of Britain, so they battled them on some issues while making alliances with them in others, resulting in a volatile relationship. The mountainous areas of north Wales became a center of Celtic life for some time because the rough terrain and bad weather in the area made it difficult for an invading army to attack and conquer the tribes, protecting them from the contentious Romans and other invading enemies, such as competing tribes hungry for resources. Because of this, Celtic tribes began to trickle away from the mainland to the Island of Anglesey, off the northwest coast of Wales, which the Romans called Mona. It keeps that name today in Welsh as Ynys Môn, or Mona Island. Here, the Romans left them to their own devices rather than try to sail across the tempestuous Cymyran Strait and the Irish Sea. This meant that the Celtic and Druidic way of life continued to survive in Anglesy until Christianity enforced its influence on the region.

By 500 BC, the Celts had spread out to inhabit southern Germany, Austria, Switzerland, and Hungary, and a hundred years later they also occupied Spain, Italy, the Balkans, northern Europe, and the British Isles. While the ancient Greeks called them *Keltoi*, the Romans knew them as Gauls, or *Galli,* which implied "barbarians" in an ancient form of Latin. The Celts were known as fierce warriors with formidable armies—so warlike, in fact, that they successfully sacked Rome in 390 BC and again in 280 BC, and desecrated the shrine at Delphi, which the Greeks considered the center of the world. In a way, their success became their undoing because they were spread over a large area, which meant that over time they became noticed by stronger enemies, principally the previously scorned Romans.

The Scottish Celts were known to the Romans as Picts, another term meant to belittle and intimidate until it was eventually widely adopted by a certain confederation of Scottish tribes. The Picts were notably tough-skinned and hard to conquer, as Scotland is mountainous and very cold in winter, making invasion difficult and the soldiers tolerant of strife. The Romans gave up the unequal task of trying to subdue the Scots and in 120 AD they built Hadrian's Wall near what is now the border between England and Scotland. This meant that the Gaelic language, and Scottish beliefs and way of life, continued to survive in Scotland.

Although a topic of much debate, it is speculated based on early Roman literature that the northern Scottish warriors, the Picts, painted their bodies entirely blue for battle using a dye called woad. The term Pict is derived from the word *Picti,* meaning "painted ones."

Once the Romans had defeated the Celts, much of the Celtic language and lifestyle began to vanish, only clinging on in peripheral areas of Europe. Celtic dialects survive in Ireland, in Scotland, Wales, and Cornwall in the UK, Brittany in France, and Galicia in northwestern Spain. A strong oral tradition helped to keep the history and mythology of these people alive, and the Druids, bards, and ovates were particularly crucial in passing on knowledge, history, and culture. Tribal chieftains and war leaders did their share of educating, but the Druidic tradition of bards and the *filí*, otherwise known as the ancient Irish poets and seers, passed on stories, legends, myths, and historical facts to each succeeding generation. The Celts were forced to move from place to place due to harsh weather, food availability, and invasion, so they had no fixed political center or power base, as did the Romans in Rome and the Greeks in Athens. Because of this, oral traditions were essential to maintain Celtic cultural identity, and they continue to be vital in preserving the culture to this day through Neo-Druidry and the stories of myth.

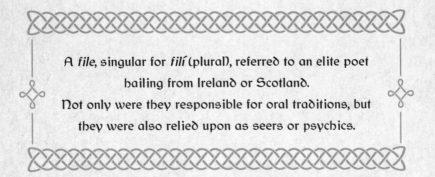

A *file*, singular for *filí* (plural), referred to an elite poet hailing from Ireland or Scotland.
Not only were they responsible for oral traditions, but they were also relied upon as seers or psychics.

While historical records can get a bit muddy and contentious across different schools of thought, we know that the Romans wrote about the Celts and Druids, often somewhat disparagingly, and produced much of what we know about the ancient Celts today. But by the seventh century AD, Roman and Christian monastic scribes were also recording Celtic stories and legends, and the influence of Celtic mysticism is clearly seen in religious rites of such Christian religions as Catholicism. The strong themes of life after death and a wonderfully peaceful hereafter sat well with the Christians, while at the same time the Celts were persecuted for what was considered to be pagan ideology.

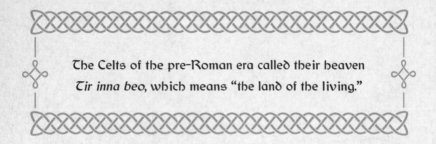

The Celts of the pre-Roman era called their heaven *Tir inna beo*, which means "the land of the living."

The Gauls have now long gone but Celtic descendants are still evident in Ireland, Scotland, and Great Britain, and they continue to perform ancient dances and rituals passed down through succeeding generations. The Breton people in the northwest region of France still celebrate festivals that link back to Celtic times, even wearing traditional Celtic hats called *coiffes*. Made from regional handmade lace, these hats showed a person's skillful craftsmanship and style.

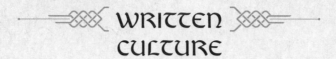

WRITTEN CULTURE

What little survives of written documentation of the Celtic way of life is evidenced through the stone carvings and scars of the Ogham carved into tools and trees. Even though the dialects of the various Celtic tribes have not survived through modern use, there is a clear correlation between ancient and modern words that show the influence of the Celtic language across several regions and languages.

CELTIC-BASED LANGUAGE

Often, the Celts had regional dialects in their language. This chart shows examples of the similarities in language that can be found across different regional tribes.

LANGUAGE	CELTIC-BASED WORD	MODERN WORD
Welsh (Wales)	Bont	Bridge
British and French	Pont	Bridge
Welsh	Llan	Field
Cornish	Lan	Field
Welsh	Dinas	Castle
Cornish	Dinas	Castle
Old Irish	Macc	Son
Old Scottish	Mac	Son

Celtic languages also have a strong influence on how we speak today. The below chart uses Irish Celtic words and shows how they are still in use today, mainly through pronunciation rather than spelling.

IRISH CELTIC WORDS
THAT INFLUENCED MODERN ENGLISH

ENGLISH WORD	MEANING	DERIVED FROM	PRONOUNCED
Shamrock	A clover	seamróg	SHAM-rogue
Slew	A large quantity	sluagh	SLOO-ah
Phony	A fake	fáinne	FAWN-ya
Bother	To annoy	bodhraigh	BOW-ra
Banshee	A screeching spirit	Bean Sidhe	BAN-she ta
Hooligan	A troublemaker	houlihan	HOLLOW-han
Galore	An abundance	go leor	GA-lore

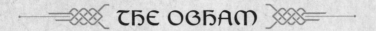
The Ogham is a Celtic script that originated in Old Ireland but there is some evidence that it was also known across Scotland and Wales, likely due to tribal migratory patterns. It is known as the Tree Alphabet, as each symbol is based on a specific sacred tree that held great spiritual power. This alphabet has been and is still used in Druid practice, making important appearances in rituals, text, and magic.

OGHAM ALPHABET

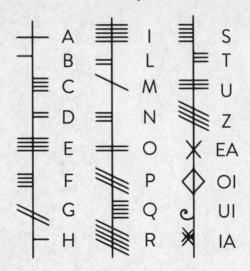

The Ogham was generally used most frequently in Ireland and Wales. Dating back to the fourth century AD, the alphabetic characters are each composed of a single vertical line representing the trunk of a tree, with diagonal lines intersecting the "trunk" as offshoots and symbols. The Ogham is still used by practitioners and is often found on authentic modern Celtic or Irish jewelry and magic tools.

Since Ogham is based on old Irish, not every one of the typical Latin characters have equivalents; there are only 20 represented. J, K, V, W, X, and Y are missing from Ogham, but luckily have phonetic replacements.

MISSING CHARACTER	REPLACEMENT CHARACTER	MISSING CHARACTER	REPLACEMENT CHARACTER
J	G	W	UU
K	Q	X	Z
V	F	Y	Y

Since we're replacing Latin characters with Ogham characters instead of translating between different languages, this conversion would be a transliteration.

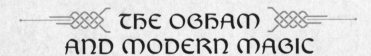

THE OGHAM AND MODERN MAGIC

One of the most common forms of Celtic magic is using the Ogham characters to enhance the power of any magical tool or place. The letters of the Ogham link to the names of trees to spiritual qualities. It is evidenced that carving Ogham characters on such things as wands, weapons, tree trunks, and stones (to name a few) brought great and directed power to any practice. For example, the Druid's staff was a wooden stick that they used for magic, divination, and to fight off enemies, and it was common that Ogham characters were carved

MAKE YOUR OWN
OGHAM STAFF OR WAND

While modern Druids have been clear about anyone not in the order attempting to perform their practices without proper training, we can still make our own staff or wand using the magic of the Ogham and the powerful attributes of wood.

1. Begin by reviewing the chart on Ogham Trees on page 24 and choose the type of wood that you'd like to create your staff or wand from.

2. Once you have chosen your wood, obtain a piece that is approximately 6 inches (15 cm) long. Remove the bark from both ends of the stick and gently sand the ends to make them smooth.

3. Refer to the Ogham Alphabet chart on page 20 and choose the letters you'll need to create a marking on the wood that is relevant to you specifically.

4. Using a wood-burning kit, a carving tool, or a permanent marker, place your personally meaningful Ogham symbols on your staff.

WRITING YOUR NAME
IN OGHAM

When learning about a culture for the first time, writing in their alphabet is a good way to make a deeper connection to who the people are. The Ogham is written in a vertical line, from the bottom to the top. Make sure you have one solid vertical line, the intersecting lines are facing the correct direction, and the diagonal angles are at consistent angles. Refer to the Ogham Alphabet chart (page 20) and the below examples for clarity on getting started. Then, grab a pen and paper and try your own name.

CHASE   RYAN*

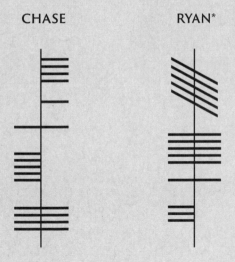

As noted on page 21, certain Latin letters are not present in the Ogham, so the character for I is used as a replacement for Y in the above example. Ryan is in fact a variant of the Gaelic name Rían.

into these staffs in order to boost and cement the power. As you work your way through these spells, rituals, and recipes, I encourage you to choose a tree whose properties you'd like to manifest in your magic and find creative ways to incorporate it into your practice.

ogham trees

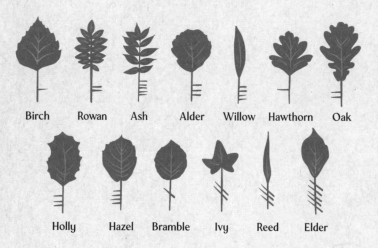

Birch   Rowan   Ash   Alder   Willow   Hawthorn   Oak

Holly   Hazel   Bramble   Ivy   Reed   Elder

ARCHAEOLOGICAL EVIDENCE OF EARLY LIFE

Physical evidence of cave dwelling in ancient Celtic times can be found through wall and stone carvings and are referred to as the Celtic petroglyphs. These images are carefully chiseled pictures that indicate not only that the Celts were there, but that they attempted to preserve their history and genealogy as early as 3200 BC. These carvings show warriors and Druids wearing conical hats while participating in rituals, including animal and human sacrifices made to Brigid, the Goddess of Fertility, and the Sun god, Lugh—both of whom were equally worshipped. There are also depictions of horses, as horse riding appears to have been essential to the Celts in their daily life as well as in war; although the most common method of transport seems to have been by water and by foot along riverbanks. Spiral designs are common in these carvings, denoting that they were sacred and meaningful symbols. A good example of this is Newgrange in Ireland, near modern-day Dublin.

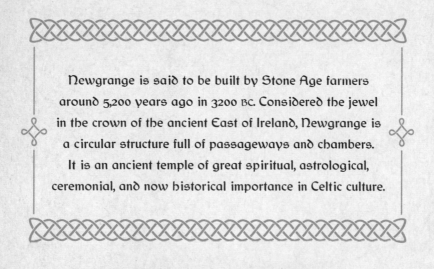

Newgrange is said to be built by Stone Age farmers around 5,200 years ago in 3200 BC. Considered the jewel in the crown of the ancient East of Ireland, Newgrange is a circular structure full of passageways and chambers. It is an ancient temple of great spiritual, astrological, ceremonial, and now historical importance in Celtic culture.

An artistic rendering of an ancient Celtic spiral symbol carved in stone in Newgrange.

From these carvings, contemporary researchers have surmised that life was short for men, and even more so for women—there was an incredibly high death rate among young females, likely due to poor nutrition and childbirth complications. Bodies have been found buried en masse with their jewelry and charms alongside them. The men were thought to be fair-haired, tall, and muscular, an assumption based on portrayals in Roman art and in the literature of Celtic slaves captured in war who worked in salt mines, as salt was a vital commodity for the preservation of food. Archaeologists have also discovered elaborate bronze artifacts decorated with solar symbols and portraying battle scenes with mounted warriors. Depictions of everything from simple domestic life to hunting scenes featuring warriors with exaggerated phallic displays have been discovered, offering illumination on early life dramas. Some illustrations are hard for us to understand in our modern context, but it is widely agreed upon that these are related to genealogy, historical records, rituals, and dances, as well as women in childbirth.

In Lombardy, Italy, thirteen "galleries" of stone carvings have been discovered, and in Germany, jewelry thought to be related to rituals has been uncovered. The pieces show beautifully intricate Celtic designs that seem to originate from southern Europe, possibly influenced by the ancient Gauls, illustrating a variety of motifs, shapes, and even faces, some of which are part human and part animal.

A depiction of an ancient Celtic ring dating back to approximately the fourth or fifth century BC. The artifact can be viewed in Gallery 301 at the Metropolitan Museum of Art.

ANCIENT LIFE

Classical writers and researchers assert that thousands of Celts travelled southward from central Europe around 400 BC, possibly due to an increase in population in northern Europe, or possibly due to a change in the climate, both of which would have impacted the availability and abundance of resources. It is speculated that brutal battles broke out over increasingly scarce resources and livable territory, resulting in whole villages being burned to the ground. Whatever the truth, it seems that the population was growing and warfare was endemic, motivating the Celts to travel to new lands to find a supportive and sustainable home. This migration assisted in the mingling of Celtic cultures across geography and once again added new depth and influence on language and ancient mythology.

The Celts were well known to love leisure and excess. The wealthy were typically buried with large quantities of gold, but commonfolk Celts also enjoyed luxuries brought north from the Mediterranean. It's possible that this love of gold and luxury contributed to their problems by draining their economy, thus motivating the young, healthy men to move out and seek their fortunes elsewhere. This disposition is likely the origin of myths such as the Irish pot of gold that can be found at the end of a rainbow.

The Celts built small settlements with houses that were square or rectangular, but most often circular. In winter, heat was provided by an open fire and, as their homes did not have a chimney or even a hole in the roof, the smoke simply seeped through the roof thatch. These buildings could withstand bad weather conditions, and their thatched sloping-roof design is still effective today in modern home architecture. Their walls were made of *wattle*—stakes or poles interwoven with twigs and branches—and *daub*, which is naturally impermeable due to mud, or other water-repellent substances like sap, being smeared across the surface of the roof to deflect moisture.

Sheep and cows were the principal livestock, while wheat was in such abundance that it was exported across the continent of Europe. Food must have been readily available a good amount of the time because the Celts were known to be robust and at least two or three inches taller than the Romans, whose average height was around five feet six inches. However, the Roman soldiers were very disciplined, and, when on patrol, didn't drink alcohol or eat meat, whereas the Celts drank alcohol owing to their love of excess and celebration, and meat was part of their staple diet, providing protein-built muscle. Deer make solid appearances in Celtic myths and legends from all regions, as they were essential to the survival of the tribes and the strength of the warriors, and, therefore, mightily revered.

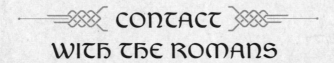

CONTACT WITH THE ROMANS

During the Gallic Wars, the Gauls were eventually defeated by Julius Caesar in 52 BC in Alisia, above the present-day village of Alise-Sainte-Reine in France, where the Celtic leader, Vercingetorix, made a fatal error: Both armies had been trailing each other up and down the Somme River and both were extremely tired, so Vercingetorix allowed his men to leave the battle lines before replacements could be brought in. Julius Caesar exploited this weak point, overtook the Gauls, and won the battle, creating a domino effect in population decline.

Upon Caesar's arrival in southern Britain, the prominent tribe at the time was the Catuvellauni, later superseded by the Trinovantes. While tribes either joined the Romans or resisted their conquest, one virtuoso led a massive revolt against Roman rule in AD 60 or 61, the Celtic Queen Boudicca.

QUEEN BOUDICCA

Boudicca, also referred to as Boadicea, was a queen of the British Iceni tribe, and her uprising is considered nobly and bravely fought, making her a Celtic folk hero. Her husband, Prasutagus, ruled as an ally of Rome. When he died, he left his kingdom jointly to his two daughters and the Roman Emperor. However, the terms of the last will and testament were ignored and Prasutagus's kingdom was annexed, and his property seized by the Romans he had once so faithfully allied with. During this betrayal, Boudicca was imprisoned and flogged, and her daughters beaten and raped. Any money she and her people had was confiscated and added to the Roman coffers.

Having trained as a warrior, Boudicca led a multi-tribe rebellion against these Roman injustices in an attempt to regain her rightful throne. While her rebel army did notable damage to various regions, including modern-day London, alas, the Roman army was ultimately much too big and better equipped. As defeat became imminent, she and her daughters chose to take their own lives rather than endure any more of the brutal treatment they were being subjected to.

Ultimately, the Romans never managed to subdue the whole of Britain. The Decangli tribe, who lived in Wales and the West Midlands, never gave in to Roman pressure, so in those regions the Celtic and Druidic ways of life persisted and endured.

GHOSTLY REMINDERS OF THE PAST

While written records of Celtic life were virtually nonexistent before the Roman invasions, there is enlightenment to be found through untangling the Celtic beliefs from the intertwining ideologies of the colonizers. The "enemies" were the record keepers, so the perspective of written records was that of the victors. It can be difficult to determine what information is purely their interpretation of the mysticism and behavior of the Celts, or their own imposed ideas and assumptions, but there are enduring ways we can begin to understand. Some of these are embodied in holy texts written by Christian monks that integrated Celtic culture.

THE BOOK OF KELLS

There are a number of exquisite books that followed the Roman era, most notably the ninth-century Book of Kells. The Book of Kells is a manuscript of the Christian Gospels, originally written in Latin, illustrated with Celtic motifs and symbolism. The name originates from the Abbey of Kells in County Meath, Ireland, currently bordered

by Louth to the northeast, Dublin to the southeast, Kildare to the true south, Offaly to the southwest, and Westmeath to the west. Christian monks were known at the time to record ancient Celtic legends and myths and incorporate those elements into their own stories. The Book of Kells is one of their most highly prized tomes.

THE MYTHICAL PERSONA

One of the most well-known characters in the Celtic myths recorded by Christian monks was Dagda. Dagda was portrayed as a Druid king and father figure, and is a representation of masculinity and strength, fertility, agriculture, and wisdom. He is a most powerful figure from whom countless mythological personas are born.

Additionally, Mórrígan was a foundational figure in Celtic myths. Also referred to as Morrígu, and in modern times referred to as Mór-Ríoghain, she is known as The Phantom Queen. It can be speculated that these iterations inspired the more common name, Morgan. Mórrígan was most commonly seen as the goddess of war and a guardian of the Celtic people and land. She finds her place of honor in the Mythological Cycle, one of the four main 'cycles' of early myths and legends. Her persona has laid the groundwork for many Celtic myths, including both male and female deities. We will discuss both in more depth in chapter seven when we discuss Celtic deities.

BELIEF SYSTEMS

Druids are considered to have been an integral part of the Celtic and Gaullist culture in Europe, with one of the first classical references to them mentioned by Julius Caesar in the first century BC. According to the Romans, Druids were polytheistic, having both male and female gods and sacred figures, in the same way that the Romans themselves once had before the dawn of Christianity. During this time, it appeared that one of the reasons for the attacks by the Romans was that Emperor Tiberius disapproved of the human sacrifices that the Druids practiced. This is a curious thing for a Roman emperor to criticize when one considers the sacrifices of Christians and gladiators in their arenas at that time. In the second century AD, Druidry seems to have begun a decline in popularity, and theories suggest that a combination of disease, famine, and destruction by the Romans (or other tribal warfare) wiped them out almost entirely.

Polytheism is the belief in more than one god. The Celts believed in many gods and goddesses, each character holding properties that led to understanding Celtic perspectives on war, famine, fertility, and all aspects of survival of the tribe.

Modern religions have often absorbed the qualities of the ancient theologies, and there is strong evidence that Christianity and its denominations, Wicca, and paganism have all been influenced by Druidry and Celtic ideology. For instance, the trinity, or number three, was considered significant in Celtic and Druidic lore, symbolizing any iteration of the concepts of strength, eternal love, and unity. While recording their new beliefs as they transitioned into what is now Christianity, early monks and priests wrote in depth about the concept of the Holy Trinity: Father (God), Son (Jesus, the Earthly form of God), and the Holy Spirit (the Creator spirit through which all things were made, in popular interpretation). Circles were a key symbol in many Druid beliefs as well as pagan thought, such as the circle of life and the Wheel of the Year, as expressed by the seasons.

These symbols were integral to Druidic rituals and ceremonies, while the lay population used them to tell stories or adorn jewelry. Druid places of worship were in secluded areas such as clearings in forests called groves, stone circles like Stonehenge in England, or near the Tree of Life (see page 149), the central tree of the tribe.

Modern-day Druids consider summer solstice to be of the greatest power, when the Sun god is crowned as the King of Summer, signifying death and rebirth. There are ritual dances performed and songs sung, but they also bring scraps of material representing things that hold them back in life and cast them to the ground to denounce them symbolically.

AN INTRODUCTION TO THE OAK KNOWERS

The Isle of Ynys Môn, referred to by the Romans as Mona, is known to have been a significant Druidic site. Now called Anglesey, and located off the coast of northwest Wales, this was a place where Druids studied and congregated once the Celts migrated there after the Roman subjugated southern Britain in around 1000 BC. It is said that to truly learn the intricacies of the Celtic cultural myths, magic, and lore, the course of a Druid's education took a minimum of twenty years—but more commonly a lifetime—since they had to commit it all to memory. All aspects of Druidism were well structured and ordered into a hierarchy; for instance, they wore colored robes according to their Druidic class: the arch-Druids wearing gold, the sacrificers (or Druidic warriors) in red, the priestly ovates donned white, the bards clad in blue, and novice students wore brown or black.

Their role was similar to that of Christian priests insomuch as connecting the people with the gods. However, it differed in the sense that a Druid could make the introduction between a human and the Otherworldly gods and goddesses, while a Christian priest was a direct mediator to God, acting as an interpreter of messages between God and the individual. Arch-Druids also acted as judges, teachers, scientists, healers, historians, and philosophers. Druids were extremely revered and respected, to the point that they had the power to banish people from society for breaking sacred laws. The Druids were also exempt from paying taxes. They were consulted to talk with the dead, see the future, and predict weather patterns for crop planting. Women were of equal standing to male Druids in many ways, uniquely allowing them to divorce, to fight in wars, and heal the sick.

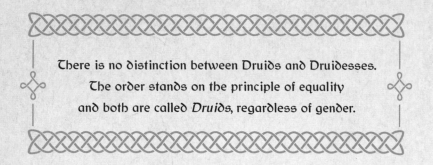

There is no distinction between Druids and Druidesses.
The order stands on the principle of equality
and both are called *Druids*, regardless of gender.

In ancient times, Druids were known as "wise elders" and would congregate specifically around oak trees as a source of power. In fact, the word Druid in ancient Celtic translates to oak knower. Julius Caesar described them, for the most part, as civilized, wise, and noble people, with the exception of alleged rituals of human sacrifice. He claimed that the Druids sacrificed criminals, the sick, and those injured in battle by putting them into massive wickerwork effigies and setting them on fire. The Druids and their congregations believed that the resulting ashes fertilized crop soil and brought prosperity to all, especially during famine. We will dive deeper into Druids in the next chapter, as they are the very foundation of Celtic mysticism.

TREE MEDITATION

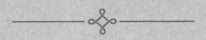

Aside from the intuitive few, many people don't really notice trees that often. They tower around us, bring us oxygen and life, and even bring us food, yet they often go unnoticed and unacknowledged. Not by the Druids! The Celts and Druids considered trees to be sacred entities that held great power, wisdom, and doorways to the Otherworld and the divine. While practitioners perform rituals and spells with trees, laypeople can conjure the same respect for these giants and appreciate their majesty through meditation.

1. Take a long nature walk. Really pay attention to the natural world around you. Look at everything, every detail, and notice the trees. Once you find a tree that strikes you as special and exceptionally beautiful, take a comfortable seat below it.

2. Close your eyes and take three long deep breaths as you feel yourself sink deeply into the ground and your body become relaxed.

3. Visualize yourself at the start of a path that leads into a beautiful forest and begin to walk to it. Feel the warmth of the sun on your back.

4. As you walk this path, imagine that you come to a large, mighty, ancient tree. Notice that its root system digs deep into the ground until it touches the Earth's core. Then observe its tall branches reaching into the heavens and through the clouds so that you can't see where they stop.

5. Now visualize the trunk. Examine its bark swirls and the scars of time. Imagine a portal of light opening in the trunk. Ask for a message from the divine.

6. Listen closely, your intuition will tell you what wisdom the trees have in store for you.

CHAPTER 2

BARDS, OVATES & DRUIDS

The ancient Celts considered bards, ovates, and Druids to be of "exceptional honor." While all three orders can be found in relation to each other, they are in essence very different.

- Bards are singers and poets: creators, artists, storytellers, poets, musicians, historians, and performers.
- Ovates are diviners and natural philosophers: prophets, clairvoyants, herbalists, tree workers, and students of natural cycles who also studied healing and protection of the Earth.
- Druids are chiefs, and the authority on moral philosophy: ritualists, teachers, counsellors, judges, and walkers between worlds.

While there are instances of crossover among the three, it's broadly thought to be an unusual combination to be of two, or even three, orders at once, so it is rarely practiced. Take, for example, the modern game of Dungeons & Dragons in which you can choose to be one of several characters, including a bard *or* a Druid but rarely, if ever, do players choose to be both.

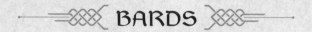

The bards passed on tradition and history orally through poems, songs, and stories that recorded and celebrated the deeds of key figures, genealogy, and notable events. They were also responsible for keeping the oral traditions of mystic folklore alive. Because of this, they played a highly valuable part in adding to and passing on tribal history. They used their verses to chastise, censor, and put to shame people from all sections of society, including the king himself at times. It was through these stories that bards showed people how to behave properly and how to "be Celtic" in culture and practice. Therefore, bards can be considered to be the "stabilizers" of society. Lucan, a Latin author, refers to bards as the national minstrels of Gaul and Britain. Remember the fili? These are the bards.

Although the official fili eventually disappeared from most Celtic regions, they survived the test of time throughout Ireland and Wales— the Irish bard through the preserved tradition of poetic eulogy, while the Welsh order of bard survives through the celebration of *eisteddfod*, an annual gathering of poets and musicians.

Training to be a bard was an intense program and lasted for several years. Of course, there were variations on their role between Ireland, Scotland, and Wales due to cultural differences, but they all underwent a similar curriculum:

- In the beginning stages of their training, a bard progressed from Principle Beginner, known as Olliare; to Poet's Attendant, or a Tamhan; to Apprentice Satirist, or Drisac. It was during this period of time that they learned the basics of spoken grammar, the Ogham tree alphabet, and at least twenty stories. Here, they carried a bronze branch to represent their status. These branches were covered in bells so that the people could hear the bards as they entered, signaling to all to settle down and be quiet because some important entertainment was on its way in. The bells were also a signal to summon the help of the ancestors and spirits of the inner realm to assist in telling the story with a magical element.

❧ For the next four years they focused on learning ten stories per year, more intricate verbal grammar, diphthongal combinations (combining two vowels in a single syllable, such as the word *coin*), and the Law of Privileges.

❧ In the sixth year they were referred to as a Pillar, or a Cli, and studied a further forty-eight poems and twenty more stories. For the following three years, they were called a Noble Stream, meaning that "a stream of pleasing praise issues from him and a stream of wealth to him." During this time, they studied the patterns of rhythm and sound used in poetry, prophetic composition, poetic forms, and the place-name stories of Ireland.

❧ The final three years of study were dedicated to becoming an Ollamh, or as we might say today, "a doctor of poetry." They learned one hundred new poems and went deeper into composition and form.

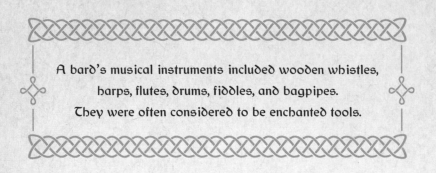

A bard's musical instruments included wooden whistles, harps, flutes, drums, fiddles, and bagpipes. They were often considered to be enchanted tools.

Bards were well-respected central figures in the community who could perform rituals and ceremonies including weddings, funerals, and baby-naming rites. They understood the eight phases of the Wheel of the Year (which we will discuss in the next chapter), and any seasonal celebrations the tribe might hold.

Noteworthy bards:

- Orpheus is often cited as being the first recorded bard (Greek mythology). He had a famous lyre which Apollo later used.
- Coirpre Mac Etaíne (Cairbre) was an Irish bard whose satire was said to be powerful enough to cause the Fomorians, a supernatural race in Celtic mythology, to lose their courage and morale during the Second Battle of Mag Tuired.
- The most famous bard of all is known as Taliesin, from Wales. He was so popular that many others have attempted to copy his oration style. This was particularly so during the great bardic revival in eighteenth and nineteenth centuries.

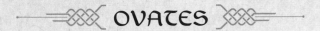

The next level of the order was the Ovates: the spiritual "shamans" of the ancient Celtic world. They were the seers and soothsayers, the time travelers, the healers, midwives, and herbalists. They could speak to the dead, and were known as the "interpreters of nature." The word *ovate* has been used in various forms by classical writers and may derive from the Indo-European root word of *uat*, meaning "to be inspired or possessed." They could use such things as the shape of the clouds, the weather, and the behavior of birds and animals to predict the future. The people relied on their knowledge of herbs to heal them (and their livestock), which is thought in some circles to be the source of the practice of witchcraft that was developed as the ovates were forced underground by Christianity. Up until the 1930s, ovates could be found actively practicing their craft in villages in Britain, where they were lovingly referred to as Cunning Folk.

The Realm of the Ancestors, which held valuable tribal wisdom, was where certain ovates focused most of their magical efforts. They were responsible for consulting with ancestors that still awaited reincarnation, and it was to them the ovates could turn for guidance on behalf of the tribe. They also concerned themselves with matters of the afterlife and answered important spiritual questions like what life after death and cultural morality should look like.

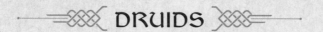

DRUIDS

Druids can be thought of as the chiefs or CEOs, if you will, of the order of Druids, bards, and ovates. They were the most thoroughly educated of the three and nothing less than judges, teachers, advisers to royalty, scientists, inventors, alchemists, peacemakers, philosophers, and spiritual guides. Their education was said to last from twenty years to an entire lifetime. If a bard was the musician and poet, and ovates the doctors and psychics, then Druids were the authority on all things related to the imparting of knowledge, both in the physical world and the spiritual realm. While certainly not priests, they did have similar duties when it came to teaching forms of worship; however, since they are an Earth religion, as opposed to the more rigid Christianity or other organized religions, they were more than just mediators between the individual and the divine.

- ❦ **JUDGES:** In Celtic society, Druids were considered to be "the most just of men," often weighing in with final decisions on personal and political disputes. They arbitrated acts of war and were exclusively responsible for making judgments on extreme cases, such as murder.
- ❦ **TEACHERS:** Druids were relied upon to teach the lay-people forms of worship, ceremony, and magical skill. They also knew a great number of verses, which helped them to teach history, genealogy, notable historical events, war, and culture.
- ❦ **ADVISORS TO KINGS:** Popular at court among kings and war chieftains, they held a high position. It is said that when a king must impart news to his court, often the Druid would speak first.

✻ **SCIENTISTS AND INVENTORS:** There is ample evidence that Druids were inventors and relied on scientific principles. For example, they constructed sacred stone circles that required measuring, calculating, and knowledge of the Sun's path, of astrology and engineering, which is all evidence of an understanding of medieval astrology and engineering.

✻ **ALCHEMISTS:** Historical artifacts and accounts from Julius Caesar tell us that ancient Druids worked with fire and metal. Working with metals gave the tribe weapons, efficient tools for harvesting, and created the beautiful Celtic jewelry that many metalworkers recreate today.

✻ **PEACEMAKERS:** Druid philosophy is rooted in peace. Druid leaders were exempt from service in the army, never carried weapons, and often mediated warring tribes.

✻ **PHILOSOPHERS:** While we know that Druids study natural philosophy, they were also concerned with moral philosophy. In this field they are not so much teachers as much as up for hearty debate. Druidry does philosophize but it is influenced heavily by environmentalism and holistic thought.

✻ **THE INNER SAGES:** While the bards open themselves up to their creativity, and ovates are the explorers of time and the power of trees, herbs, and animals, the Druids channel their inner Sages. A Sage, or wise person, is the philosopher and counselor who judges and teaches. In tune with their advanced wisdom that surpasses the wisdom of the bards and ovates, they are the highest of the Order and the most revered.

MODERN BELIEF SYSTEMS AND NEO-DRUIDRY

Although an ancient practice, there are still groups that employ Druidry today, and they're relatively easy to find with a quick internet search. One of the most established is the Order of Bards, Ovates, and Druids, and they are not only a group of practitioners, but also a school where, once you've committed, you can learn to be a Druid. This is a worldwide group of over twenty-five thousand members that spans over fifty countries. Curious about becoming a Druid? This is a great place to start. The Order was founded in Britain by the poet Ross Nichols, with contributors such as Vera Chapman, a writer and founder of the Tolkien Society. They are heavily influenced by the Ancient Druid Order, which came into being from the Druid Revival, about three hundred years ago. This order is derived from the magical traditions and ancient foundational principles, rather than orders of pure academic study.

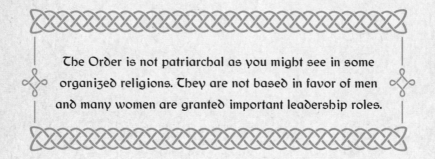

The Order is not patriarchal as you might see in some organized religions. They are not based in favor of men and many women are granted important leadership roles.

COMMITTED MEMBERSHIP

As proponents of peace, even in modern times, Druids tend to function within a spirit of acceptance and love. When seeking membership, the Order is happy to accept people from all walks of life, regardless of gender, sexual orientation, ethnic origin, and even unsavory pasts. With a central philosophy of tolerance and inclusiveness, and a strong focus on compassion, they reject all harmful notions. They refuse to scar the human spirit with damaging philosophies that perpetuate sexism, homophobia, and racism. The very essence of their philosophy places modern-day Druids alongside civil rights activists, anti-animal cruelty groups, and environmentalists. The Druid's Prayer, also called the Gorsedd Prayer (see page 56), emphasizes the virtues of compassion and respect for all life, celebrating its beauty and diversity with a strong bond to community. It inspires the knowledge and love of justice, the love of all existences, and Druids seek to embody this with their preservation of spirit and Earth. Modern Druids gather to sing and tell stories, recite poetry, and celebrate the seasons and sanctity of life through retreats, gatherings, camps, conferences, and workshops.

Before the 1960s, Druids had seemed to all but disappear from the modern world, the few remaining being of Welsh and English origin. But disputes arose even between the two dwindling groups, and they distanced themselves from the spiritual aspect of the practice, focusing mainly on academic study. That is, until George Watson MacGregor Reid (approximately 1850-1889), a vocal proponent of Druidic practice, spoke up and proposed that spirituality be incorporated back into the practice and urged people from all faiths to learn and join their ranks. His philosophy, which he called the Universal Bond, resuscitated the power of the ancient Druids and Revival Druids alike.

MAGIC-INFUSED IRISH SODA BREAD

In the spirit of the Druids, who use plants and herbs to fortify their food and health, try this easy and quick Irish soda bread recipe. Soda bread uses sodium bicarbonate, more commonly referred to as baking soda, as a leavening agent rather than yeast. To qualify as traditional Irish soda bread, the recipe must contain baking soda, buttermilk, flour, and salt. With these simple ingredients, it's likely that the breads of the ancient Celts were similar in construction and taste. This is delicious served warm with butter, fruit jam, or honey. It's also wonderful along side soups and stews, as it mops up the broth beautifully. It is likely that ancient Celts made a version of this bread to fortify their diets with wheat and grain, and was served alongside a cauldron of stew.

For the Druidic touch, I like to use rosemary as the fresh herb, which symbolizes love and remembrance for those who have passed, but it's flavor isn't for everyone, so you can use an herb or a combination of herbs of your choice. A good combination is parsley, chives, and sage; but you can also look up the symbolism of different herbs so that the magic of the bread suits your needs. Make sure their flavors work well together. Nobody wants to eat ginger basil lavender bread!

Ingredients:

- ❧ 2½ cups (315 g) all-purpose or whole wheat flour
- ❧ ½ cup (40 g) dried oats
- ❧ 2 teaspoons baking soda
- ❧ ½ teaspoons salt

- 2 cups (200 g) walnuts, chopped (This is optional. I like the flavor of nutty breads, but if it's not for you, replace this with 1 cup, or 240 g, of shredded cheddar cheese.)
- ¼ cup (120 ml) cooking oil (soybean works nicely)
- 1 teaspoon honey
- ¼ cup (60 ml) buttermilk
- ½ cup (18 to 35 g) chopped fresh herbs

Instructions:

1. Preheat the oven to 350°F (175°C; gas mark 4) and lightly grease a 9 x 5-inch (23 cm x 13 cm) loaf pan.
2. In a large bowl, mix the flour, oats, baking soda, salt, and walnuts until combined.
3. In a medium bowl, whisk together the oil and honey.
4. As you continue to whisk, add in the buttermilk and herbs until combined.
5. Using a wooden spoon to stir, add the wet ingredients to the dry ingredients until combined in a gooey dough.
6. Place the dough in the prepared loaf pan and bake in the oven for 1 hour, or until toasty brown on top and until a wooden toothpick, when stabbed in the center of the loaf, comes out clean.

This recipe adds herbs to a traditional Irish soda bread recipe, but in place of herbs, you can also add nuts, caraway seeds, raisins or other dried fruit, and even chocolate chips!

CAULDRON
OF ABUNDANCE

Boiled beef stew would have been a popular and familiar meal to the ancient Celts. Ingredients dropped into a roiling pot of water to cook were thought to be transformed magically by the boiling water, and friends and loved ones gathered around to share. Cold storage wasn't a thing back then so it would all have to be eaten in one sitting. These days, it is a good idea to cook a quantity of stew, allow it to cool and put some in the freezer to make a quick meal when you need one. You need a slow cooker (mine is called a Crockpot) or a large oven-safe cooking pot.

Ingredients:

- 1 tablespoon vegetable oil, plus more if needed
- 2 pounds (907g) beef chuck roast, cut into 1-inch (2.5 cm) cubes, fat and gristle trimmed
- 1 large yellow onion, sliced
- 3 cloves garlic, minced
- 5 large carrots, sliced
- 1 pound (454 g) baby Yukon potatoes, skin on and cut in half
- 1 teaspoon cornstarch
- 3 cups (720 ml) water
- 2 cups (480 ml) beef stock
- 1 teaspoon salt
- ¼ teaspoon black pepper (optional)

You can add some pieces of other vegetables that you have on hand, such as cauliflower, cabbage, peas, and so on. Add these faster-cooking vegetables in the last 20 minutes of the stew's cooking time to soften them.

Instructions:

1. In your pot, heat the oil over medium-high heat until it sizzles. Add the meat to the pot and brown it on all sides.

2. If needed, add a bit more oil to the pot, then add the onion, garlic, and carrots and cook and stir until the onion starts to become translucent. If the garlic starts to burn, reduce the heat to medium.

3. Add the water, beef stock, and cornstarch. Stir to combine, then bring to a simmer.

4. Add the potatoes, salt, and pepper. Stir to combine, then let simmer on low for 5 to 6 hours (more if necessary), until the potatoes are soft and meat is cooked through.

5. Serve in deep soup bowls with old-fashioned bread, such as soda bread, artisan bread, or something of the kind.

Beer is a traditional accompaniment to stew and in the past, people often drank low-alcohol beer because it was safer to drink than water, which often came from a dubious source, so you might like to keep to tradition by drinking some low-alcohol beer with this meal.

Eat, drink, and think of your link with the Druids and the Celts.

Even if you don't feel called to join an order, it's still possible to embody the principles by which Druids live. Link up with nature, spend time in it, learn about the landscape, flora, and fauna in your region. Become an environmental crusader and contribute to nonprofit organizations that focus on kindness to the Earth, animals, and people. Try minimalizing your consumerism, relying only on the basics, recycle and repurpose as much as you can, tend to a garden, watch a sunset in quiet contemplation without your headphones, eat healthy and organic foods, and try to live by the Druidic Code (see page 67). There are countless ways by which you can give an appreciative nod to Druidry through your own, everyday actions.

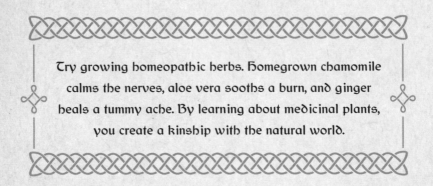

Try growing homeopathic herbs. Homegrown chamomile calms the nerves, aloe vera sooths a burn, and ginger heals a tummy ache. By learning about medicinal plants, you create a kinship with the natural world.

If you don't feel ready to commit to any of these practices just yet, you can also simply live by the notion of helping others. The Ancient Order of Druids—another of the largest international groups of Neo-Druids—is known to take tithes much like a modern Christian church, but rather than spend that money on their church building or other luxuries, they save this pot for when a member of their congregation has a crisis or has to take a significant amount of time off work due to illness. The concept of brotherly love is a central focus across all Druid organizations. There are many ways you can practice this aspect of Druidry in your daily life. Have you seen the same person asking for spare change on a busy street corner? Offer to buy them a warm meal or a hot cup of coffee. Call your friends to genuinely ask how they're doing. Offer a bit of financial help to a struggling friend. Speak kindly to all, avoiding harsh judgments and words. Volunteer your time and give back to your community. Do not spread gossip or betray secrets.

Another foundational concept of Druidry is kindness to the Earth. The Celts and Druids relied heavily on the natural world around them for everything from sustenance to divine insight. All of life on Earth was revered and appreciated for the unique gifts they provided. Of particular importance were herbs for healing, water as a source of life, deer and other animals as sustenance and as spiritual symbols whose behaviors could make futuristic predictions, and trees as gateways to the divine. Caring for the health of the Earth was essential to the survival of the tribes and the individuals who comprised them. Neo-Druidry leans heavily on environmentalism and preservation of natural resources. Here are some simple ways you can incorporate being kind to the Earth in your everyday life:

❈ **WALK MORE.** Although it might seem like a small gesture to take a ten-minute walk to the store rather than a two-minute drive, each time you decline to start your car, the fewer carbon emissions there will be. Imagine the impact it would have if hundreds, or even thousands committed to this.

❈ **REUSE AND REPURPOSE WHAT YOU CAN.** This may take some creativity at first, but to get started you can do things like rinse and dry your ziptop bags between uses (which will also save you money), save empty pasta sauce glass jars for food storage (which also helps to organize your kitchen cabinets), or cut an old t-shirt up into reusable face wipes or dust rags.

❈ **SAVE WATER BY BEING CONSCIENTIOUS ABOUT HOW AND WHEN YOU USE IT.** Stop leaving the water running while you brush your teeth, only turning it on when you need to rinse, (which could potentially save up to about twelve liters of water while you brush), shave a few minutes off your shower time, and only run the dishwasher when it is packed full. Try washing smaller items by hand.

❧ **WATCH FOOD WASTE.** The more food that decomposes in a landfill, the higher the levels of methane gasses invade our atmosphere and air. Stews, casseroles, and one-pot meals are a great way to repurpose leftover food (and save a little money). If you're feeling ambitious, you can start a composting project.

❧ **TURN OUT THE LIGHTS EACH TIME YOU EXIT A ROOM.** It's easy to forget you even have a light on if it's daytime, so double check when you enter or exit a space.

❧ **STEP AWAY FROM FAST-FASHION.** According to the UN Environment Programme, the fashion industry is the second-largest consumer of water aside from agricultural industry, and is responsible for approximately 10 percent of global carbon emissions on the whole. The rise of mass-produced, trendy items is forcing these numbers skyward. Investing in well-made clothing reduces the amount of fashion waste you might be responsible for.

❧ **MAKE YOUR HOME MORE ENERGY EFFICIENT BY INSTALLING LED LIGHTBULBS.** LED lights have a life expectancy of approximately five times that of regular bulbs and use less energy. Try also sealing all the cracks around your windows and doors to avoid drafts. It will pay, both literally and figuratively, to keep the house cool in the warmer months, and warm during the cooler time of the year.

THE DRUID'S PRAYER

The Druid's Prayer was first recorded by Iolo Morganwg (Edward Williams, 1747–1826) and updated in modern times, is commonly used by Neo-Druids:

Grant, O Great Spirit/Goddess/God/Holy Ones, Thy Protection;
And in protection, strength;
And in strength, understanding;
And in understanding, knowledge;
And in knowledge, the knowledge of justice;
And in the knowledge of justice, the love of it;
And in that love, the love of all existences;
And in the love of all existences, the love of Great Spirit/Goddess/God/
Holy Ones/the Earth our mother, and all goodness.

DO YOU HAVE WHAT IT TAKES TO BE A DRUID?

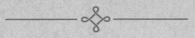

Answer the following questions in this quiz to see whether you would make a good Druid.

1. Do you believe in a sacred relationship with nature?
2. Do you seek to understand the divine link between ourselves and our ancestors?
3. Are you open to learning how you can be more accepting and tolerant of others?
4. Are you interested in rituals to honor the Earth, trees, culture, heritage, ancestry, and the seasons?
5. Are you willing to reframe your beliefs that might've been learned through organized religion?
6. Do you find it exciting to learn about oral traditions, spells, and ceremonies?
7. Are you into all things organic?
8. Do you draw strength from a strong sense of community?
9. Are you concerned about our planet and climate change?
10. Are you interested in learning about the power of holistic medicine and herbal healing?

If you've answered eight out of ten of these questions with a *yes*, I encourage you to look deeper into Neo-Druidism. It might be a place where you find a spiritual home and like-minded people.

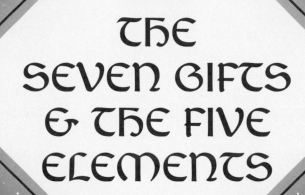

CHAPTER 3

THE SEVEN GIFTS & THE FIVE ELEMENTS

In modern times, the term Druid refers to a wide assortment of spiritual paths and practices, all of them rooted in ancient tradition and nature-based spirituality. It is a timeless art, as Druidry seeks strength and healing through its relationship with the Earth and natural world. As touched on earlier in this book, ancient Druids were physicians, astronomers, musicians, poets, philosophers, legislators, and judges of the people, as well as educators in religion and spirituality. Not much has changed philosophically since the days of closely guarded forest rituals, as the list of modern practitioners of Druidism is longer than you might think. As we grapple with global warming and environmental preservation, it can be said that anyone who considers themselves an environmentalist is dabbling in Druidry.

With over two millennia of history backing them, modern Druids—or Neo-Druids, as they are commonly referred to—differ only slightly from their ancestral practitioners. Neo-Druids embrace the foundational concepts, connect intimately with nature, and have a focus on spirituality and academic study. In 2001, the American Religious Identification Survey showed that out of over two hundred million people interviewed, approximately thirty-three thousand considered themselves Druids. They don't have structured or weekly church services as you might see in modern organized religions, but they do have rituals and prayers that are universal to all sects of Druidry.

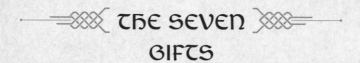

THE SEVEN GIFTS

The most widely known Druidic organization is the Order of Bards, Ovates, and Druids. Considered to be a modern authority on Druidry, this congregation presents the Old Ways in a modern context, seeing ancient wisdom as a treasure chest brimming with valuable knowledge and leadership. The Order sums up these treasures in seven main "gifts."

THE FIRST GIFT: PHILOSOPHY

This Druidic philosophy places the sanctity of the natural world and our connection to it above all else. It emphasizes the sacredness of all life and leans on the principles of an ecological, geocentric, pragmatic, idealistic, spiritual, and romantic world view.

THE SECOND GIFT: A RELATIONSHIP WITH NATURE

The order believes that, above all else, to be in touch with the divine you must have an active relationship with the natural world around you. They set their minds to physically working with plants and trees, interacting with animals, appreciating the grand displays of the seasons, and pausing to consider even the smallest stone.

THE THIRD GIFT: HEALING

Neo-Druids focus on healing and rejuvenation though physical practices geared toward promoting health and longevity. This can simply mean being conscientious about how you treat your body—eating nourishing, organic food, exercising regularly, and getting plenty of sleep.

THE FOURTH GIFT: THE JOURNEY OF LIFE

To honor life as a journey, Druids ritually and symbolically celebrate each of life's milestones. The path they walk is lined with rites of passage and are acknowledged through rituals including the naming of children, marriage, death, and other forms of initiation from one phase into another.

THE FIFTH GIFT: THE OTHERWORLD

The Otherworld can sound ominous, but in reality it refers to techniques for exploring other states of consciousness outside of our day-to-day perceptions. These higher planes and other realities are explored through meditation practices and rituals that open up a spiritual plane of existence with a far bigger reach than what our physical minds can easily comprehend. To explore and understand your place outside of your human body is a gift indeed.

THE SIXTH GIFT: OUR POTENTIAL

Current Druidic practice offers guidance on a path to self-development. To err is human and being human is a progressive lesson that leads to opportunities to improve. This gift focuses on one's potential to become a better version of themselves. It recognizes our creative potential, our intuitive abilities, and fosters intellectual and spiritual growth.

THE SEVENTH GIFT: MAGIC

While Druids do practice magic through spells and rituals, this gift refers more to the art of being open to the magic of being alive. This refers to that special, supernatural ability to manifest our dreams and desires, seek our own unique wisdom, and provide others with healing and inspiration.

A common misconception is that Druids worship idols, the devil, or practice Satanism. None of this is true and all are falsehoods likely perpetuated by early Christians seeking to eliminate competing ancient theologies. Because much of their inner workings are done privately and only amongst themselves, assumptions and misconceptions have bombarded and warped the Druid image in the public eye for centuries.

HEALING WITH HERBS

Herbs are still widely used to help relieve the aches and pains that life can bring. Try turning to one of these the next time you have an issue you might need to address. Nature works in tandem with advances in science and technology, so consult with your doctor before adding any herbal remedies to your healthcare routine.

HERB	PROPERTIES	HEALS
Garlic	Antiseptic Antibiotic Antiparasitic	Poor digestion High blood pressure High cholesterol
Fennel	Anti-inflammatory	Poor digestion Menstrual cramps Mental health
Aloe Vera	Anti-inflammatory Antiviral	Sunburns Skin wounds Weak immune system
Ginger	Anti-inflammatory Antioxidant Medicinal	Poor digestion Nausea Morning sickness
Ginseng	Anti-inflammatory Antioxidant	Fatigue Erratic blood sugar Slow brain function
Chamomile	Anti-inflammatory Antioxidant	Anxiety Insomnia Restlessness

HONORING
THE ELEMENTS OF LIFE

As we've learned, Druids value their relationship with nature above all else, so it makes sense that they also lean heavily on the five elements in their philosophy: air, fire, water, earth, and spirit. Aside from carving out time to perform a spell or ritual, here are some ways you can apply the Druidic perspective in your everyday life using their symbolism.

AIR

Ruling the east, this element is represented by a hawk, and it involves communication, objectivity, knowledge, reason, fairness, freedom, new beginnings, and learning. To connect with the element of air, sit outside on a day when there are a few clouds in the sky, then allow yourself to relax and fall into a slight trance. Watch the clouds and see if they make patterns that have something to tell you.

FIRE

Ruling the south, this element is represented by the stag, which denotes energy, passion, power, sensuality, drive, and creativity. To connect with fire, light a candle and sit at a bit of a distance from it, then gaze at the flame and see if you can tune into things that are happening in your life reflected in the flame.

WATER

Ruling the west, water is represented by the salmon, and it indicates intuition, emotions, healing, rest, spirituality, and connection with all things. Sit by the sea, a lake, a river, or any natural body of water and ask the water to speak to you. Envision your mind being washed clean of all negativities.

EARTH

Ruling the north, earth is represented by the bear, which suggests grounding, stability, connection with the earth and the home, prosperity, and steadfastness. Stand outside somewhere with bare feet on the ground and ask the earth to give you protection and comfort. Hone in on the feeling of the ground beneath your feet. Really *feel* the force of gravity connecting you to the ground.

SPIRIT

While considered an element of life, spirit isn't always denoted when the elements are discussed. This is mainly due to the different interpretations of the sacred elements across Celtic regions. Spirit, also referred to as Nwyfre (pronounced "Oh-ir"), is derived from the Welsh term that refers to the essence of life that flows within each sentient being. This refers to your consciousness, your own unique spirit that acts as the driving force of your life path.

THE DRUIDIC ELEMENTS
AND THEIR PROPERTIES

The chart below shows a casual interpretation of the properties and powers of the Celtic elements. There are scores of volumes written about these sacred elements and what they meant to the Druids, in particular and I encourage you to dig deeper.

ELEMENT	PROPERTIES	RITUAL
Air	Intellect, thoughts, ideas, creativity, introspection	Spring equinox
Fire	Warmth, passion, action, strong will	Summer solstice
Water	Emotion, intuition, spirituality, ancestors	Autumn equinox
Earth	Grounded to the world, home, security	Winter solstice

THE DRUIDIC CODE

We've touched on the ancient and modern Druid philosophy, but let's break it down in their own words. Neo-Druids live by eleven codes of conduct based on ancient Druidic teachings, and while these act as a spiritual oath, they are also principles that every modern individual, not just Druids, should practice if they want to live a life of respect and peace.

1. Every action has a consequence that must be observed, and you must be prepared to compensate for your actions if required.

2. All life is sacred, and we are all responsible for seeing that this standard is upheld.

3. You live in society, and you must always respect others.

4. Hold yourself and the work that you do to high standards.

5. Make an honest living.

6. Always be a good host, as well as a respectful and grateful guest.

7. Fuel your body with healthy food, drink water, take exercise, and sleep.

8. Serve your community. Volunteer, help someone across a busy street, pay it forward, and encourage others.

9. Maintain a healthy balance of the physical and spiritual. As you care for your physical being, also nurture your spirituality through meditation, prayer, or preferred practice.

10. Uphold the truth, including being truthful with yourself.

11. Take care when expressing your convictions, particularly when judging or accusing someone, but also when debating.

As you read through this list, take note of which you currently live by and how. Are there items that you feel you might be lacking in? Consider how you can begin to incorporate these concepts more into your daily life, even in small ways.

THE MAGICAL SIGIL

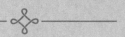

A sigil is a powerful magical symbol that is created with a lot of thought and intention. Used for centuries by Druids and Wiccan practitioners, the term sigil refers to a sign, mark, seal, or symbol that holds strong intentions and power. There are many ways to create sigils, to empower them, and use them in magical practices. It's unclear where Druid sigils originated, but the most common today is the below Druid sigil.

This symbol is said to be the symbol of Druidism and it represents the Earth Mother. In ceremonial magic of old, sigils call on the power of gods and goddesses, represent the sovereignty of the natural world, or are linked to powerful spirits. Today, sigils aren't usually employed in the same way they were in ancient times but are used to conjure strong intentions and can be used for a multitude of reasons: Manifesting dreams, protection, love magic, or bringing luck, to name a few.

CREATING A SIGIL

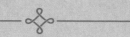

1. The first thing you'll want to do is set an intention for your sigil. As an example, let's say you feel like things have been a bit precarious lately and you feel that your intuition is telling you to protect your home from negative energy. You would set your intention as *protection*. Other examples might be love, passion, good luck, prosperity, good health, and so forth.

2. Decide which materials you want to use to create your sigil. A pen and a piece of paper work perfectly fine, but you can also inscribe this in wood with a wood-burning kit or a carving knife for a more permanent sigil. Go with your gut.

3. Write out your intention word and delete any repeating letters. Using our protection example, the word would now be precin, since we eliminate the repeating t and o.

4. Now, remove the remaining vowels: Prcn.

5. Using the remaining letters, create a symbol by calling on your imagination and intuition. Once you have your symbol, either write it on a piece of paper or a block of wood. Be sure to keep your intention in mind as you do this.

6. Depending on the type of modern magic being practiced, what you do next could vary. You can hold the sigil in your closed hands to warm it with intentions before burying it underneath a special tree, post it near the doorway of a home, use in crystal grid magic, or burn it while saying an intention aloud. The choice is yours!

CHAPTER 4

THE WHEEL OF THE YEAR

The Wheel of the Year is a set of holidays that align with the changing seasons and with Earth-based practices. Essentially, it functions as a calendar that focused solely on the cyclic change of the seasons and marking the Sun's course through the sky. The major festivals are marked by Samhain (October), Imbolc (February), Beltane (May), and Lughnasadh (August). These are celebrated in tandem with the solstices and equinoxes. Referred to as the "quarter festivals," these include midwinter, also known as Yule in December, Ostara in March, midsummer in June (also called Litha), and Mabon in September. The health of the crops depended on the Wheel of the Year by informing when it was time to sow, plough, and harvest. The turning of the wheel represents the ever-eternal cycle of life: birth, death, and rebirth. If you want to follow this Druidic calendar, then you'll have to make adjustments specific to your region and hemisphere to fit your local farming activities. In this chapter, we will discuss the celebrations and holidays on the Wheel of the Year, as practiced by the Celts.

THE CELTIC YEAR

For Druids, the year has a mythic context, equating the cycle of growth, the seasons, and the progress of honoring the goddesses and gods throughout the year. The Wheel of the Year and its seasons is symbolic to new beginnings, there is no stopping and starting but a seamless flow of the growth of the annual cycle through all of the festivals.

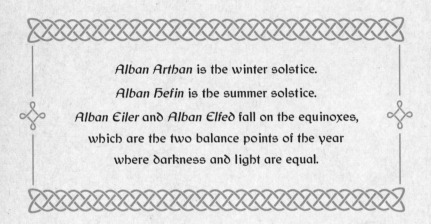

Alban Arthan is the winter solstice.
Alban Hefin is the summer solstice.
Alban Eiler and *Alban Elfed* fall on the equinoxes,
which are the two balance points of the year
where darkness and light are equal.

The Druids used (and still use) this wheel of time to determine when seasonal celebrations would take place to honor the gifts given by the natural world and its own cycles of life. Much of their philosophy is based on this interpretation of the yearly cycles: a set of eight holidays every seven weeks. The Wheel includes the two equinoxes, the two solstices, and the four fire festivals. The Latin *equi* means equal, and *nox* means night, indicating that the equinoxes are of equal night and day lengths. The solstices are a different story. Summer solstice (June 21) marks the longest day of the year, while winter solstice (December 21) signals the shortest day of the year.

Four celebrations that are known as Solar Festivals mark the seasons, while the Fire Festivals are also known as the Cross-Quarter days, and these are agricultural festivals. These Festivals mark the dormant and active stages of agriculture, and each is ruled by a deity that Druids honored with rituals to ensure success for their crops and animals during the coming year.

THE DRUID WHEEL OF THE YEAR

SAMHAIN
OCTOBER 31

The Samhain festival marks the end of harvest season and the beginning of the "dark season," or winter. The festival celebrations are typically held on the evening of October 31 and stretches into November 1, as the Celtic day started and ended at sunset. Samhain falls between the autumn equinox and winter solstice. Here, the Celts would button down for the winter: The harvest is done, food has been preserved and stored to sustain the tribe throughout the cold months ahead, and the time for hibernation and rest begins. In modern day, this is a good time to reflect; to come to terms with our faults and flaws and find ways of rectifying them. It is also a time for reviewing our lives and clearing away all that's no longer needed.

Pagans who embrace Celtic traditions and who intend to reintroduce them into modern practices are called Celtic Reconstructionists. In their tradition, Samhain is referred to as *Oiche Shamhna* and it celebrates the mating between Tuatha Dé Danann, and the gods Dagda and River Unis. Pagans also celebrate Samhain by placing juniper around their homes, and by creating an altar for the dead where a feast is held in their honor. Many years ago, bonfires were lit to protect the family and the land through the winter darkness, and torches were set ablaze to honor the dead. These days, incense is burned, candles or lamps are paced in windows, and quiet reflection on friends and loved ones who have passed away begins.

ALBAN ARTHAN, WINTER SOLSTICE, YULE
APPROXIMATELY DECEMBER 21

Alban Arthan is a fire festival that occurs on the winter solstice and welcomes the rebirth of the Sun. This is an important turning point because it marks the shortest day, after which the light will gradually start to increase until the summer solstice. Now is the time to acknowledge all that has gone before and is no more. This festival's modern name is Light of Arthur. To this day, celebrants still hang up mistletoe at Christmas, which falls a few days after the solstice. It is interesting to note that mistletoe used to be excluded from church decorations, due to its connection with the Druids and its pagan and magical associations.

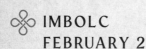 ## IMBOLC
FEBRUARY 2

Imbolc is another of the fire festivals and it celebrates the initial signs of spring—when the first ploughing occurs and the sowing of crops is initiated. This festival celebrates the passing of winter and the start of the agricultural year. Imbolc is also known as Candlemas. It is the day on which we honor the rebirth of the Sun and honor the Celtic goddess, Brigid. She is also known as a triple goddess, so here she is worshipped for all her aspects. During this time, Druids give themselves and their land spiritual healing, and pagans recognize this holiday as one of reflection, rejuvenation, and new beginnings. Pagans and Druids usually focus on the cleansing element of water during this holiday.

✤ ALBAN EILER, SPRING EQUINOX, OSTARA
APPROXIMATELY MARCH 21

Alban Eiler marks the spring equinox, when day and night are of equal length. It is the second of the spring festivals and its concerns are around fertility, as this is the time when seeds are blessed for planting. This festival is also known by its modern name, Light of the Earth. You can use this time to free yourself from things that hinder your progress, so it is a good opportunity to perform spells that help you banish bad habits or negative thoughts and emotions.

✤ BELTANE
APRIL 30 TO MAY 1

Beltane is the third of the spring holidays and it is also known as the Celtic May Day. Beltane celebrates sexuality, life, and unity. This is the season for love, wedding vows, ceremonies, and commitment, so it is a popular time for hand-fasting, a pagan marriage ceremony. It's the time of final sowing and planting, and of sending the cattle out to summer pasture. In ancient times, rituals were performed to promote fertility, and cattle were driven between twin fires for good luck and to protect them from illness. Some of these Druid rituals became absorbed into Christianity, so the early outdoor ceremonies were later held in churches, followed by a procession to the fields or hills.

✤ ALBAN HEFIN, LITHA, SUMMER SOLSTICE
APPROXIMATELY JUNE 21

This holiday celebrates the warmth of the Sun and the bounty of summer. This is a great time to gather herbs for magical or cooking purposes. This festival is also known by its modern name, Light of the Shore. In ancient times, the summer solstice was often marked with torchlight processions, which entailed setting fire to tar barrels or wheels bound with straw, which, once aflame, were rolled down steep hillsides. It was believed that this practice, done on the summer solstice, would bring fertility to crops and livestock, and prosperity to the people. People would dance around fires that were, and still are, known as balefires, where brave souls leap through the flames as a purifying or strengthening rite.

LUGHNASADH, LAMMAS
AUGUST 2

Lughnasadh is the fourth fire festival and the festival of the first harvest. It is a time for meetings, contracts, swaps, trades, and exchanges. Here we begin to reap all that we have sown in both practical and metaphorical terms, while the vegetables ripen. There are many traditions and customs all over the world that are carried on at harvest time, but in the old days, it was a time for bread making. Activities to enjoy during Lughnasadh would be walking through the woods to spend time meditating in beautiful surroundings. This is also a celebration in honor of the Celtic god Lugh.

ALBAN ELFED, FALL EQUINOX, MABON
APPROXIMATELY SEPTEMBER 21

During the autumn equinox, the wheel turns and balance is restored. This is the time of the second harvest, typically of fruit trees. It is during this time that the ceremonies center around gratitude to the Earth for her abundance, her motherhood, and her generosity to the tribes.

It is through these celebrations that many Druids and Wiccans maintain a close relationship with the Earth and its seasons. This is what they turn to in order to recognize and show appreciation for what the seasons offer—in ancient times, wisdom and survival; in modern times, wisdom and splendor. They offer a sense of balance and are a physical representation of the passage of time. According to the Druid's Garden blog, the following are ways that you might celebrate these holidays.

- Celebrate by performing grove rituals, sharing food with loved ones, or focusing on companionship.
- Build outdoor or indoor shrines or establish an altar for the season.
- Plant or harvest herbs, fruits, leafy greens, etc., or establish a garden.
- Engage in various bardic arts such as wildcrafting, painting, music, or writing poetry.
- Donate your time to others and the environment, such as participating in a group environmental clean-up.
- Celebrate the holidays through personal ritual (it might be really useful to you to create your own meanings and ritual celebrations for each holiday).
- Meditate, reflect, and engage in divination work.

SAMHAIN RITUAL

While there are established rituals that are practiced by people who follow the Wheel of the Year, these can take years to learn and a commitment to a practice to perform. But there are ways to honor the seasons without dedicating your whole life to a specific practice. If you wish to connect to Samhain, the Celtic New Year, follow the below instructions for performing a ritual.

1. Perform this ritual on November 1.
2. Begin by choosing a special candle. Since Samhain marks a new year, refer to the list of elements and choose one that carries the properties that you wish to infuse throughout your new year. Then choose your candle color based on that: red for fire, blue for water, yellow or white for air, and brown or green for the earth. Samhain marks the returning of the sun, so the flame of the candle represents the sun.
3. After you've lit the candle, write on a piece of paper all of the things that you do not wish to bring with you into the new year. Looking back over your life since the last November, did you find that you had a lot of conflict with your family and feel that you'd like to see things from a new perspective? Write it down. Do you have a bad habit you want to let go of? Write it down.
4. Meditate or sit in quiet contemplation of change, endings, and new beginnings.
5. Keeping fire safety in mind, roll the paper into a tube and ignite the end. Release all that you want to let go of as the paper burns. Safely discard of the ashes.

CHAPTER 5

DRUID TOOLS, SYMBOLS & KNOTS

There are thousands of legends that reference Druids, sages, and oracles, and some of these stories mention their tools or the items they carry with them. It was believed that a Druid's tools held great power, and many mythical stories are the result of this magic. These tools were not used against people, but to enrich their lives through applied magic. The Druids often carried their tools with them for quick access should they need to perform a rite or spell in order to help someone. They were also commonly used as divination tools, meaning objects that helped them to communicate with the divine in times of rituals, tribal insecurity, fortune and future telling, and ceremonies. Symbols were often carved into the tools to bolster their power. Ogham characters were carved on wands and staffs, cauldrons, tree trunks, stone, and the handles of sickles and knives, believing that the characters could summon the power of the sacred trees that they represented.

DRUID TOOLS

SICKLE

A Druid's sickle is also known as a crescent sickle, Druid knife, the Celtic knife, the ritual blade, and the foraging blade. This sickle is hand-forged with a spiral handle and a crescent-shaped blade made from a single piece of iron. Druids used it to cut mistletoe and medicinal herbs in the sacred woods under the moonlight. This 8-inch (20 cm) crescent-shaped blade is sharp on both the inside and the outside edges, and when it's not in use it is stored in a leather sheath. It is also used as a ritual knife that is kept on an altar.

CRANE BAG

A Druid's crane bag is a magical kit filled with objects such as shells, rocks, feathers, stones, Ogham letters, representations of the elements, ritual tools, and much more. The term "crane bag" comes from the Irish mythology of Manannán mac Lir, a major sea god who is also the guardian of the Otherworld. His crane bag was said to have been originally crafted from the skin of a crane, hence the name. The myth is that this bag was full of his many treasures: his knife and his shirt, the shears of the King of Scotland, the helmet of the King of Lochlainn, the bones of Assal's swine, and the girdle of a whale's back, along with magical birds, hounds, and other things. His bag also contained the human language, a powerful tool and often a weapon in its own right.

In the modern Druid tradition, Druids create magical bags of their own, and the contents of each crane bag is unique to each Druid. It is an expression of the person and their path, so modern Druids may carry wands, a small sickle, something to represent the elements, and a notebook in their crane bag.

POWER OBJECT BAG

It's also more common to have a smaller crane bag, one that is small enough to fit in a pocket, around a person's neck, under clothing, or attached to a belt. It contains objects significant to the modern Druid, such as sacred stones, shells, sticks, herbs, teeth, bones, or other powerful items. The person's energy and connection become stronger while the bag is carried around, and the objects inside the bag lend their strength, power, and protection to the individual throughout the day.

FIELD BAG

This bag would contain offerings, knives, folding saws, matches, and more that could be useful when foraging for wild foods or medicinal plants, when camping or engaging in bush craft, or for other kinds of wild crafting. It can also hold tools used for protection, wands, a small cauldron, or food.

COMBINATION CRANE BAG

This bag is a combination of all those mentioned previously, but with a few personal items and ritual tools added in. The benefit of this is that the Druid ends up with a multipurpose bag that can serve many needs. Modern crane bags are made of any durable material, such as linen, wool, cloth, denim, and the like. It is possible to buy a pre-used crane bag, but many modern Druids prefer to make their own, as that infuses their own personal energy into the tool.

WAND

The wand is one of the most recognized of all the items, and it is a very personal tool that is used to direct personal power. The Druid may choose a particular type of tree that would give a specific result when used in a ritual, but a wand should never be cut from a living tree. Wands were enhanced by carving Ogham letters or other symbols into them or by adding a crystal to the tip. This is a personal tool that should not be handled or played with by others.

STAFF OR ROD

Staffs are often made from wood, but it is a matter of personal preference as to which wood is chosen to create it. The staff is generally between three and six feet long, and while it is used for protection, it can also be used for marking out space for rituals or for measuring things, including bodies when preparing them for burials. It is said that in ancient times the staff was also used to keep a record of journeys by marking the wood with small notches.

EGG

A Druid's egg is made from stone, crystal, or any other suitable material that comes from the natural world, and thus represents the element of earth. This serves the purpose of grounding, so practitioners hold this in their hands during meditation to bring focus and balance. Stone is a more common choice for this purpose because stone is said to contain old wisdom from the earth, and it also has the effect of making the practitioner patient.

CORD

This cord's primary function is to lay out sacred spaces or outline sacred geometry. It is typically a piece of cord that is at least twelve feet in length with knots tied at one-foot intervals until there are twelve total knots. This is considered "knot magic," and it is achieved by focusing the practitioner's intent into each knot, therefore tying the knots and the intent to the Universe.

BUILD YOUR OWN
POWER OBJECT BAG

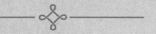

A staple of any Druid's arsenal of tools, the power object is one of the few tools whose sole purpose is to engage with the person who carries it. They are typically filled with talismans chosen specifically and carefully by the Druid as a source of spiritual energy that they can carry throughout the day. Many people already have a version of this: do you have a special box that holds sentimental objects that you can revisit when you feel like you need a boost of happiness and warm feelings of nostalgia? The ability of these objects to spark good feelings is a testament to their spiritual power. Druids wore (and still wear) these bags as a powerful reminder of what makes life meaningful to them, and a constant access to the positivity they bring.

- �֍ Start by thinking about and gathering your power objects: lucky charms and sentimental objects that bring you a sense of positivity. These can include a small picture of yourself or someone that you feel encourages you, a lucky coin, a worry stone, crystals whose power speaks to you, herbs and flowers that carry the qualities you seek, a special shell you once found, meaningful pendants; anything that is important or represents what is important to you.

- ✖ Place them in a bag that you can wear around your neck, tie to your belt, place in a handbag, a car, or a satchel. The important thing is that you are able to keep them with you throughout each day.

- ✖ As they gain power, you will begin to feel the safety and love they bring into your life.

CAULDRONS

Energy objects played a major part in the lives of the Druids and the Celts, but so did cauldrons. There is an ancient poem from the seventh century AD that is attributed to an Irish poet called Amergin. This poem is preserved as part of a sixteenth-century manuscript, along with some material in eleventh-century language, and when modern scholars discovered it, they named it "The Cauldron of Poesy." The poem relates to stories and poems in Celtic Druidry on the subject of "three internal cauldrons." Here is a small section of "The Cauldron of Poesy":

> The Cauldron of Vocation
> Fills and is filled,
> Grants gifts and is enriched,
> Sings praises and is praised,
> Chants invocations and is enchanted,
> Creates harmonies and is harmoniously created,
> Defend and is strongly defended,
> Orients and is aligned
> Upholds and is upheld.
> Sources of nourishment
> Objects of quest
> And containers of transformation.

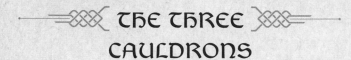

THE THREE CAULDRONS

The cauldron was an important tool in early Celtic life, symbolizing fertility, abundance, and rebirth, while also being utilized for most domestic tasks, such as cooking, boiling, carrying water, and bathing. It was a crucial element of Celtic social life, as gathering around a cauldron to eat and break bread together was a common way to maintain connections within the community. But they also played a vital role in rituals, rites, and Celtic magic. The basis of the magic is thought to be when a cauldron filled with water is placed over a fire, the water then boils (striking the ancient Celts as magical), transforming anything you drop into it (in other words, cooking it, also thought to be proof of magical powers). It is said that in the Celtic Underworld a person is granted poetic inspiration according to how hard their cauldron boils, the highest boil signaling immeasurable creativity. Cauldrons make countless appearances in Celtic mythology and are central in lore and stories, one of the most famous being Dagda's Cauldron of Plenty.

As we know of Dagda, he was a generous, fatherlike deity whose gifts to humanity were plentiful and never-ending. In turn, the Cauldron of Plenty—one of the Four Treasures of the Tuatha Dé Danann—was said to never be empty and those of good character were jovially invited by the god to eat their fill from it. This cauldron was said to be so large that two grown men could rest in the ladle.

Also of notable repute across ancient mythology are the Three Cauldrons, known as the Celtic chakras. Each cauldron represented an energy center in the body (much like Sanskrit chakras) and indicate the state of one's overall health: spiritual, mental, and physical. They also corresponded with the three realms, the Earth, the Sea, and the Sky. The concept of the three stems from the poem "The Cauldron of Poesy" by Amergin (see page 88), which describes Three Cauldrons as Coire Goriath, the Cauldron of Warming or Incubation; Coire Ernmae, the Cauldron of Motion or Vocation; and Coire Sois, the Cauldron of Inspiration or Knowledge. These are the root of all wisdom.

CAULDRON	ENGLISH NAME	CHAKRA	REPRESENTS
Coire Goriath	Cauldron of Warming or Incubation	Belly	REALM: Sea (lower realm) REPRESENTS: Physical health TIME: Past PURPOSE: Gives wisdom to youth
Coire Ernmae	Cauldron of Motion or Vocation	Chest	REALM: Land (mid-realm) REPRESENTS: Emotional and mental health TIME: Present PURPOSE: Inner growth
Coire Sois	Cauldron of Inspiration or Knowledge	Head	REALM: Sky (upper realm) REPRESENTS: Spiritual health TIME: Future PURPOSE: Gives wisdom to poetry and art

There are many symbols and icons that can be found in Celtic mythology, their religious beliefs and practices, along with emblems of gods and goddesses, images from mythological tales, and symbols of magic and spirit.

THE TRIQUETRA

The simple triangle became a complicated shape formed of three *vesica pisces* shapes, sometimes with an added circle in or around the whole. The triquetra is often found in art, metalwork, and illuminated manuscripts such as The Book of Kells.

THE ARWEN

The Arwen, also known as the symbol of three rays, is a symbol of the balance between male and female energy or between two opposing powers in the Universe. It was often used in jewelry with the three rays running parallel to each other. The first and last rays signify the powers of the male and female, while the middle ray signifies the balance and equality of the other two rays.

THE SHEELA NA GIG

These are figurative carvings of naked women displaying an exaggerated vulva. Carvings of the pagan hag-like goddess can be found on churches, castles, and other buildings, particularly in Ireland and Britain. These images were considered a form of protection that would also bring luck. The Sheela Na Gig were first carved in France and Spain in the eleventh century AD and reached Britain and Ireland in the twelfth century AD.

THE CELTIC CROSS

A Celtic cross is a symbol that combines a cross with a ring surrounding the intersection. This became a common Christian symbol but also a pagan one, which was linked to the idea of the life-giving properties of the Sun.

THE TRIPLE SPIRAL

A Celtic and pre-Celtic symbol found on many Irish megalithic and neolithic sites, the triple spiral also appears in various forms in Celtic art, with the earliest examples having been carved on stone monuments. Later examples were found in Celtic Christian manuscripts.

THE GREEN MAN

The green man motif has many variations in Celtic mythology. He is depicted as a face, surrounded by or made from leaves, twigs, fruit, and flowers. He is considered to be a god of spring and summer, rebirth, and the growing cycle of spring. He disappears and returns each year, enacting themes of death and resurrection, the ebb and flow of life, and creativity.

In the Arthurian legend of Sir Gawain, the Green Knight had a green helmet, green armor, a green shield, and even a green horse.

THE TRISKELION

The triskelion symbol looks like a three-legged wheel and is a prominent Celtic symbol that represents the concepts of completion, progress, and advancement. It represents actions, cycles, progress, revolution, and competition.

THE AILM

The circle in the Ailm symbol is a Celtic sign that denotes the wholeness, intactness, and purity of the soul. Ailm symbolizes pure energy, integrity, objectivity, clarity, strength, and good health. Its symbol represents the branches of the fir tree, which is one of the nine sacred pieces of wood used for the sabbat fire. It also represents strength, resilience, endurance, longevity, friendship, honesty, truth, and perceptiveness.

THE CELTIC BULL

The bull had an important role in Druid sacrifices and rituals, and it was considered the symbol of no compromise, stubbornness, and strong will. The Celts have also long associated the bull with sovereignty, wealth, status, abundance, virility, and fertility. In ancient Ireland, a new High King's crowning was always preceded by a ritualistic feast of beef. For a Celtic clan or village, a good bull represented its prosperity and prestige.

THE SHAMROCK

The shamrock is arguably the most famous symbol of Ireland. It is associated with Saint Patrick, who used it to teach people the Christian concept of the Holy Trinity of the Father, Son, and Holy Ghost. It is considered to be representative of abundance, nurturing, fertility, productivity, and stability. The shamrock is said to have mystic powers because its petals stand up when a storm is approaching, warning people of the impending danger. It is also used as a charm for bringing good luck and warding off evil.

 # THE CELTIC KNOT

Celtic knots were a variety of knots used for decoration, and these were adopted by the ancient Celts, but they have long since been adapted to decorate Christian monuments and manuscripts.

THE DARA CELTIC KNOT

Dara can be traced to an Irish word, *doire*, which means oak tree. The Dara Celtic knot is associated with the root system of oak trees. The Celts, and especially the Druids, considered the oak tree sacred, and saw it as a symbol of destiny, power, strength, wisdom, leadership, and endurance.

QUATERNARY CELTIC KNOT

This knot could symbolize the four directions of east, west, north, and south; the four elements of nature, earth, fire, water, and air; or it can be associated with the four fire festivals, Samhain, Beltane, Imbolc, and Lughnasadh.

THE ETERNITY KNOT

Celtic knots represent eternity because as a series of overlapping or interwoven knots they neither have a beginning nor an end. There are many examples of the Celtic knot pattern that feature prominently in early Christian manuscripts as ornamentation.

CIRCULAR KNOTS

The circular shape of these knots emphasize the continuity of life, or eternity. Some interpret this knot as standing for the infinite quality of some object or attribute, whereas others consider it as emphasizing continuity or even endlessness. For this reason, this Celtic knot is very commonly seen in wedding rings or other gifts that lovers exchange, to represent the endless nature of their feelings for each other.

DRAW YOUR OWN
CELTIC KNOT

Try drawing a Celtic knot design:

1.

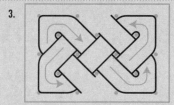

Start by creating a dot grid pattern on a sheet of paper. In the last row of dots, starting with the second dot from the left, draw diagonal lines connecting the two dots upward and to the left, extending additional lines outward from the center. Stagger your lines so they are placed above and below the dots, never through the dots.

2.

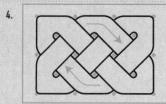

Close the lines by creating rectangles in a crosshatch pattern, alternating between placing the line above and below the dots.

3.

Following the direction of the arrows, and using the dots as your guide, create curved lines to close the crosshatch.

4.

Continue to close the pattern by following the direction of the arrows for the upper and lower center curves.

5.

Darken your pattern lines with a thick, bold marker, then fill in the center gaps. Erase any remaining dots that still show.

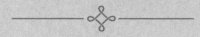

CREATE A
TRIQUETRA BRACELET

The triquetra knot has many meanings, as it is one of the most important and universal Celtic symbols. One way of looking at it is as a symbol of the cycle of one's life: birth, death, and rebirth. The meaning for this can be ascribed to your life as a whole, or any meaning that applies to that concept in your personal life. This exercise will teach you to make a triquetra bracelet for yourself that represents yourself and your life. The materials you need can be found at any craft store. For this tutorial, we use a green cord and a gold cord, but you can use any color or fabric option you prefer (see a list of material options below). Once you have your two pieces of material, label one "green" and the other "gold" with a bit of paper tied to the end to help keep track of which color goes where as you follow the weaving instructions.

You'll need:
- � Two different colors of paracord, leather, craft cord, or fabric
- ✷ Jewelry fastener
- ✷ Jewelry glue
- ✷ Small pliers

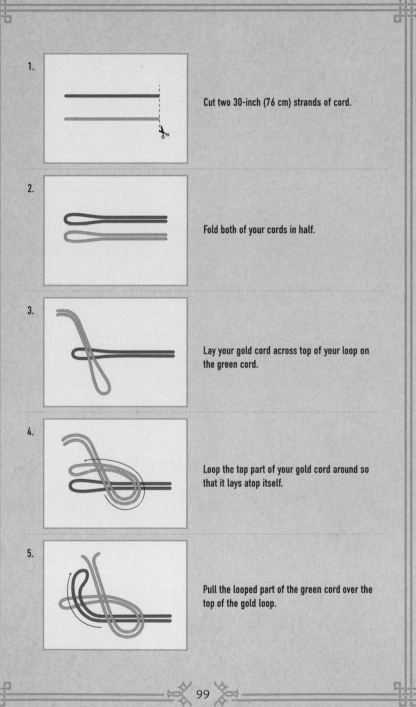

1. Cut two 30-inch (76 cm) strands of cord.

2. Fold both of your cords in half.

3. Lay your gold cord across top of your loop on the green cord.

4. Loop the top part of your gold cord around so that it lays atop itself.

5. Pull the looped part of the green cord over the top of the gold loop.

6.

Then pull the gold ends over the green loop.

7.

Grab the looped end of the green cord and place it over the gold cord, then under itself.

8.

First, tighten the knot by pulling the looped end of the gold cord, and the looped end of the green cord in opposite directions. Pull all ends until the cords tighten into a knot.

9.

This creates a central knot to go on top of your wrist and leaves two gold strands and two green strands on each end.

10.

Cover the ends with a glob of glue and allow to dry. This will prevent it from fraying.

11.

Use your pliers to fasten the clasps to each end.

Once you've tried your hand with fabric, which not graduate to harder materials?

You can use silver or copper wire to create the shapes for Celtic-style jewelry. Fashion into a thick band for a bracelet or chain, or create individual charms to wear as pendants. You can also carefully weld or glue them onto pins to make brooches. Longer pieces could be glued on to strips of leather or cloth to make different styles of bracelets or brooches. It might even be possible to use enamel for the spaces between the pieces of wire, and even to make hair clips out of the shorter rectangles.

CHAPTER 6

CELTIC MYTHS, LEGENDS & FOLKLORE

The lore of the Celts doesn't seem to be exiting our lives any time soon. On publication of this book (2023), a wave of fresh interest emerged with the popularity of such books and television shows as *Outlander* (created by Ronald D. Moore, Starz, 2014–2023). Dripping with Scottish and Irish folklore, the popularity of this show (originally *The Outlander* book series, written by Diana Gabaldon, Dell Publishing, 1991–2021) created a spike in interest in the magical legends, and Celtic mythology has been revived in pop culture yet again. You'd be hard pressed to find someone who hasn't heard of fairies or leprechauns, lucky clovers, or mermaids. The stories told since the ancient times of the Celts are irresistibly magical, with mischievous characters, portals to distant times and lands, and soulful heroes.

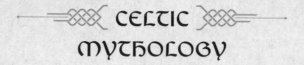

CELTIC MYTHOLOGY

As we've seen, Celtic mythology has a complex history and a rich life
to this day, which in many ways we owe to our modern Druids, bards,
and ovates who keep the stories and traditions alive. The majority of
Celtic myths hail from Ireland and Wales, but as the geographical reach
of the Celts spread throughout much of Europe, the mythology began
to morph to accommodate the influences of regional cultures creeping
in from the English county of Cornwall, Scotland, and the French
region of Brittany. Because of this, Celtic mythology is divided into four
cycles, or groups: the Mythological Cycle, the Ulster Cycle, the Finn
Cycle, and the King's Cycle.

THE MYTHOLOGICAL CYCLE

The Mythological Cycle is considered the first in the canon of cycles
and stories. This cycle details the arrival and disappearance of
the first inhabitants of Ireland. These were a group of godlike and
supernatural peoples called the Tuatha Dé Danann. Speculation about
the disappearance of these enlightened beings gave birth to mythical
creatures such as leprechauns, changelings, and the Banshee.

THE ULSTER CYCLE

The second cycle of myth is the Ulster Cycle, which is thought to have taken place during the first century—a tumultuous era for the Celts. It was around this time that the birth of Jesus Christ was thought to have occurred. The stories folded into this cycle detail quests and feats of ancient heroes, specifically in the areas of Ulster in the north, and Leinster in the south, and are heavily influenced by the religious and political strife of the time.

THE FINN CYCLE

This third cycle is an account of the hero's journey of Fionn mac Cumhaill (lovingly referred to as Finn) and his mighty warriors known as the Fianna. Written in the third century AD, this cycle also relates stories about other famous Fianna members, including Diarmuid, Caílte, and Fionn's rival, Goll mac Morna.

THE KING'S CYCLE

The final Irish mythological cycle is the King's Cycle, also referred to as the Historical Cycle. These stories relay the history and genealogy of ancient Celtic royals, as told by court poets and bards.

> The disappearance of the Tuatha Dé Danann made way for the Aos Sí, who are thought to exist in a parallel universe alongside ancestors, kings, and heroes. Tir na nÓg (the Otherworld) could be accessed near burial mounds, fairy hills, stone circles, and cairns.

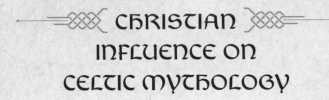

CHRISTIAN INFLUENCE ON CELTIC MYTHOLOGY

As we learned earlier, Christianity was a powerful force that steadily crept into and across the Celtic regions. While the Celts resisted their influence, the two ideologies inevitably interwove to create their individual theologies. When you think of Celtic symbols, your mind might automatically go to the Celtic cross—a Christian cross that displays meaningful Celtic knot designs. As Christianity gained steam throughout Europe, the Celts adopted the ideas that they thought were most in line with their ancient belief systems. One such example of this is Saint Patrick.

SAINT PATRICK

When hearing the name of Saint Patrick, it likely invokes memories of fun and wild Saint Patrick's Day celebrations. However modern it has become, the hints of Christianity and Irish lore can be seen in the deep Catholic roots of sainthood, and the legendary leprechaun. Contemporary celebrations aside, early Irish Christians revered Saint Patrick as a symbol of Christianity's triumph over paganism. His persona was that of a peacemaker and mediator between Christian and pagan schools of thought, rather than a warmonger and conqueror.

SAINT BRIGID

Today, those who are familiar with Ireland and its culture will easily recognize Saint Brigid of Kildare. The second patron saint of the Emerald Isle (a beautiful way to refer to Ireland), Brigid of Kildare is considered a model to look to for the vocations that were considered female-focused at the time: The care of babies, the duties of the midwife, Irish nun devotion, and the physical labor of the dairymaids. The story of Saint Brigid is rooted in the ancient legend of Brighid, one of the deities of the ancient Tuatha Dé Danann.

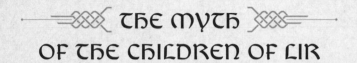 THE MYTH OF THE CHILDREN OF LIR

There are countless myths that have emerged from the Celtic mists of time and culture, but one interesting example is that of the Myth of the Children of Lir. As with all mythologies, especially those that have been kept alive by word of mouth, there are variations on the events, names, and places. Here we will stick to the most commonly accepted version of the story and keep it brief.

The story begins thousands of years ago in the time and place of the Tuatha Dé Danann; a time when warlords ruled. As war and strife churned with the invasion of the Gauls, the people felt compelled to elect a king that would protect them from these ruthless invaders.

The king they elected was Bodhbh Dearg, affectionately called Bov the Red, who was accepted by all but Lir, who wanted the kingship for himself. Lir openly refused to pledge allegiance to the popular king, causing most of King Bodhbh Dearg's supporters to declare him a traitor and insurgent, punishable by death. However, this was a forgiving and kind king who refused to prosecute Lir.

LIR'S CHILDREN

Upon learning that Lir's first wife had died after three nights of illness, the king took pity on his stricken rival and offered Lir the hand in marriage of one of his three foster daughters, but on the condition that he declare allegiance to his crown and recognize him as king. Lir was so enticed that he dropped his grudge and made the declaration that Bodhbh Dearg was king. Lir chose to marry the eldest royal daughter, Aobh ("Eve" in modern day), and she in turn brought joy to his life where sadness once reigned. Together, they produced four beautiful children—Fionnuala (the eldest daughter), Aodh (Fionnuala's male twin), and younger twin sons, Fiachra and Conn. Tragically, the beautiful Aobh died while giving birth to their youngest twin sons and Lir was devastated with grief.

Upon word of Lir's shattering loss, King Bodhbh Dearg once more offered to ease his pain through a marriage to Aobh's sister, Aoife. She proved to have a different, less practical countenance than her sister, becoming jealous of the attention that Lir showered on his children. She even feigned illness for a whole year in an attempt to draw the attention toward herself. When that proved to provide insufficient attention from Lir, Aoife concocted a plan to kill the children. At first light, Aoife ordered a chariot to take her and the children on a journey under the guise of visiting their grandfather, the king. Due to an ominous and prophetic dream the night before, Fionnuala knew that her intentions might not be as pure as they appeared and resisted embarking on the journey. But it couldn't be avoided, so off they went at dawn. About halfway into the trip, Aoife ordered the chariot to stop at a secluded location and ordered her servants to kill the children. When the servants refused to harm the sweet children, Aoife attempted to do it herself and lifted her sword to them, only to have it deflected by unseen forces, if not her own conscience. As they continued the journey, Aoife built up her nerve, and once they reached the Lake of Oaks, Loch Dairbhreach, she ordered them to go to the water to wash. Again, Fionnuala's intuition spiked and she resisted, eventually relenting. Once in the lake and distracted, Aoife, using a Druid's rod, cast a spell on the children, turning them to swans. Fionnuala desperately implored her to be kind, and being moved by the girl's desperate insistence, allowed them to keep their human speech and granted the gift of song to sing the beautiful music of the Sidhe, music that soothed troubled hearts.

THE SWAN CURSE

Although Aoife showed a tiny light of mercy to the swan children by gifting them speech and song, the curse imposed the harsh sentence of three hundred years caged by the waters of Loch Dairbhreach, then three hundred more years captive to Sruth na Maoile (the Straits of Moyle between Scotland and Ireland), and, finally, three hundred additional years at Irrus Domnann and Inis Gluaire. The sentence would be lifted only when the first bells of Christianity rang, upon the arrival of Saint Patrick. Once the curse was complete, Aoife continued on to the castle alone. When she arrived solo, the king immediately asked after his beloved grandchildren and she told him that their absence was due to Lir's resistance to them spending time with the king, a flat-out lie. The wise king refused to believe her and sent a messenger to Lir to confirm the truth. On receiving word that the children were missing, Lir set out for the castle, fearing that the children had been met with harm.

LIR'S REVENGE

While passing Loch Dairbhreach on the long trek, Lir heard the voices of his children down by the lake. Beholding them as swans, he realized what Aoife had done. Overcome with grief, Lir and his men became very upset, only comforted and lulled by the beautiful music of the swan children. Although reluctant to leave his children the next day, Lir set off for the castle, determined to tell the king what had happened. When he finally arrived, he immediately told the grief-stricken king of the curse imposed by Aoife. King Bodhbh Dearg invited Aoife to a meeting, and without yet mentioning the swan children, asked her what she is most afraid of. "The howling north wind," she answered. Upon this discovery, the king lifted a Druid's rod and turned her into a "witch of the air," who, as legend has it, still listens to the howling north wind and her screams can be heard throughout the storms.

Lir and King Bodhbh Dearg returned to the lake, only to find they could not break the curse (as we know, Druid magic is powerful!). For the next three hundred years, pilgrims from all across Ireland traveled to behold the beautiful stories and music of the swans. Too quickly, their three-hundred-year tenure at Loch Dairbhreach came to an end and it was time for them to embark to the Sea of Moyle to live out their next three-hundred-year stint as swans. Travelers and adorers of the swans were devastated at their departure, and as the Sea of Moyle was known to be a harsh and wild place, King Bodhbh Dearg decreed that no one could kill a swan in the entirety of Ireland, an offense that was punishable by death; a law that remains active in Ireland today.

THE PASSAGE OF TIME

Time passed slowly for the swan children on the Sea of Moyle, until one day they spotted a troop of riders approaching the mouth of the Banna River, which feeds the sea. Calling out to them, they united with the men, who turned out to be the two sons of King Bodhbh Dearg, Aodh Aithfhiosach and Fergus Fithchiollach. They had searched far and wide for the swan children on orders of the king, and upon finding them were relieved that they were alive and well. They stayed near to the swan children and delighted in their stories and lovely songs before returning home to report the good news.

The remaining three hundred years were spent on Irrus Domanann, a brutally harsh environment where they suffered great pain, even freezing along with the sea. It was a torturous three hundred years, but once they had served the nine-hundred-year sentence, they eagerly returned to Sidhe Fionnachaidh in search of their father, Lir. Upon arrival, they discovered that Lir had long since passed away and their childhood home was gone. They journeyed to Inis Gluaire, where they beheld the first chimes of the Christian bells, although the curse was not yet broken. News reached Saint Mochaomhog, also known as Coamhog, who immediately met the children to ask them if they were the children of Lir.

SAINT MOCHAOMHOG

Once he learned that the swans were indeed the children of Lir, Mochaomhog invited them to live with him, where they were well looked after. The King of Connacht, commonly referred to as Lairgren, and his wife, Deoch, had heard of the mystical singing swans and wanted them for themselves. When Mochaomhog refused to turn the children of Lir over to the couple, Lairgren grew furious and attempted to grab them. At the moment he placed his hands on the swans, the spell was immediately broken and they returned to their Earthly human form. As the feathers fell away, what remained was four wrinkled, time-wizened humans. Lairgren and Deoch were so terrified that they fled in horror. Ripened by time, Fionnuala realized that they were not long for this world and begged Mochaomhog to baptize them before they perished. They died in peace and were buried the way they had lived for nine hundred years, together—with Conn on Fionnuala's right, Fiachra on her left, and Aodh between her arms in a loving embrace.

Legend has it that when the children of Lir died, Mochaomhog dreamed that he saw four beautiful children flying over the lake and into Heaven. Today, the myth of the singing swans lives on through beautifully crafted silver jewelry that is exclusively made in Ireland, and is the kind of folklore that can be heard being recounted by storytellers in pubs dotted throughout the country and in children's bedtime stories. Swans are still protected by law to this day.

THE LEGEND
OF THE ONCE AND FUTURE KING

You'd be hard pressed to find anyone that hasn't heard of King Arthur and the Knights of the Round Table. From the 1963 Disney animated film *Sword in the Stone*, to Arthurian-themed restaurants, at least some version of this legendary tale still lingers in contemporary culture. But who can remember the original version? Let's recap.

Arthur's story begins with his father, Uther Pendragon. Igraine, the wife of the Duke of Cornwall, caught the eye of Pendragon. Disguising himself as her husband, he snuck into Igraine's bed, and later she conceived Arthur. Born of deceit and shame, Arthur was sent to be raised by Merlin the Wizard, who had designed the great Round Table for Uther. This famous table could house 150 soldiers and they met there to strategize the intricacies of keeping the kingdom safe. Upon Uther's death, the knights found themselves with no figurehead to turn to for guidance and unable to decide who should take Uther's place. Merlin declared that whoever could draw a mysterious sword lodged in a large stone would be the next king.

Many tried, and just as many failed until Arthur, now attendant to his foster brother Sir Kay, was sent to find a new sword to replace one broken during a practice sword fight. Unable to locate a fresh sword, he wandered into the gardens. Being unaware of the spell that Merlin had performed in order to find the new king, Arthur spotted the sword and eagerly pulled it directly out of the stone with ease. And, just like that, a Celtic king was born.

This and other Celtic mythologies talk of magic as a part of everyday life, and many of the characters practice magic or have a connection to other worlds that frequently overlap at recognized places. Most often the myths are born from real historical figures, and through time, the true stories of their kingly reigns or heroic conquests bolster them more and more until they are supernatural and magical figures.

The tale of King Arthur is an example of a king who progressed from being a mortal ruler to an otherworldly protector. He has several archetypal and elemental associations, and he can be seen as a king who ruled over a golden age. The earliest stories of Arthur came in the form of Welsh manuscripts such as *The Black Book of Carmarthen*. Chiefly a collection of poetry from the ninth to the twelfth centuries, it touched on everything from the horses of Welsh heroes to religious subjects, including also odes of praise and love, and mourning for the dead.

King Arthur was born in North Cornwall at the Castle of Tintagel, which can be visited today. Half of the castle ruins are on the mainland, and the other half are on a nearby island. Previously, there was just a simple bridge made of ropes and wooden boards connecting the two, but now a properly constructed, modern bridge links the two for safe passage.

Of greatest legend are the poems which relate to the Welsh heroes and their associations with the Old North, modern-day Cumbria and the surrounding area. Especially cherished are the tales of Arthur and Merlin.

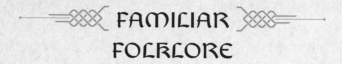

FAMILIAR
FOLKLORE

Just as the legend of King Arthur is interwoven into our modern culture, there is plenty of Celtic folklore that you're likely also familiar with.

- ✤ **SHAMROCK:** A good example of ancient folklore intermingling with Christianity, the shamrock was used by Saint Patrick to educate the Celts on the Holy Trinity: The Father, The Son, and The Holy Spirit.

- ✤ **HEADLESS HORSEMAN:** Likely a familiar story, *The Legend of Sleepy Hollow* is based on fairy mythology that claimed that dark, headless fairies were going to ride through town. If they stopped, it meant that someone in town was set to die.

- ✤ **LEPRECHAUN:** Originally known as *leath bhrògan*, the leprechaun is the cultural symbol of Ireland. This oral tradition said that when you visit Ireland you must try to find the pot of gold at the end of the rainbow. But watch out! The gold is guarded by grumpy little men who will stop at nothing to protect their stash.

- ✤ **MERMAID:** Throughout the nineteenth century, it is said that in southern Europe there dwelled beautiful women who had the tail of a fish, but in the less desirable cold water, they were said to have pig faces and fangs.

✤ **PIXIE:** The myth of the pixie is a tale of love. An Irish leprechaun named Coll falls in love with an evil fairy named Aine, disguised as a beautiful goblin. They were blissful together until the terrible empress of dark fairies cast a spell on Aine, turning her into a magpie. Desperate to have his love back, Coll asks the good fairy queen to lift the spell and she does so on the condition that he find Aine and profess his love. He happily does just that and the curse is lifted.

✤ **FAIRY:** Fairies, cousins of pixies, are likely the most widely-known mythical beings. In Ireland, they were thought to live in *cnocs agus sibhe*, meaning "mounds of earth," and can be both good and evil. They are ruled by fairy queens and kings, and are known to possess great magic, as well as mischief. Even in contemporary times, you can conjure fairies for spellwork, or invite them to your garden, as they are very beneficial to plants.

Although less common in contemporary culture, the pookah were one of the most feared creatures in Irish folklore. They were known as shape-shifters that often first appeared as a vicious dog with glowing red eyes. They could also morph into humans or goblins…whatever was needed to achieve their nasty goals.

IRISH SPELL TO ATTRACT GOOD LUCK

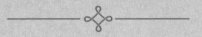

1. Start with a candle, some string, and a trinket or charm.
2. Light the candle.
3. Loop the string through the trinket and tie it in a knot.
4. Swing the trinket above the flames and chant:

As flame flickers, and this charm I pass,
good luck and blessings come to me,
wealth, wisdom, esteem, and energy.

MAKE A WISH

You don't have to wait for your birthday cake to blow out the candles and make a wish. The Celts believed that fairies were supernatural beings that had access to our world, and that they could bring luck, grant wishes, and good fortune. But these are multifaceted and complicated beings who were also said to steal children and replace them with fairies so that they could experience the love of a human child, use them as slaves, or to get revenge on someone who has wronged or attempted to harm them.

Because their characters are complex, fairy magic has a wide range of uses in the modern world. Here, you will summon the fairies and ask that they grant you a wish.

For the spell, all you need is a candle and a small bell. Fairies love the sound of music, chimes, and spells, so this is a good method for calling on them. Give an offering in return so as to maintain a good relationship with them. They also love sweet treats so a thimble of honey is always appreciated, but you can give bits of fresh fruit or sweetened nuts.

1. Begin by situating yourself in a quiet, comfortable space where you won't be disturbed. This can be either inside or outside at the base of a special tree.
2. Set up your candle on a heat-safe surface. Focus on your wish as you light your candle.
3. Clear your mind of all clutter by taking several long, deep breaths with your wish in the forefront of your mind.
4. Place your offering near the candle so that it is bathed in its light.
5. Ring your bell three times, then recite:

Lovely fairies of ageless grace
I invite you to my sacred space.
Hear my wish and accept my treat,
So that desire transpires and fairies feast.
Most joyful fae with feet petite,
Grant my wish so life is sweet.

6. State your wish out loud, then repeat the above verse.
7. Ring the bell six more times, then blow out the candle.
8. Take your blessed offering to a quiet place outside and bury it as an offering of gratitude to the fairies.

CHAPTER 7

CELTIC DEITIES

Across geography and time, the Celts, especially the Irish, were polytheistic. This means they worshipped more than one God, as some other religions do. They were thought to have a long list of over three hundred deities, but as we know, there wasn't written record-keeping during that time so it's difficult to pin down a firm number. Our current knowledge is based on what few written records we have, so there's likely a lot more to the story, especially considering that Celtic culture could vary according to region. Of the deities we're certain of, the following gods and goddesses can be found across Celtic literature, each influencing the myths and legends uniquely.

TUATHA DÉ DANANN
CHILDREN OF THE GODDESS DANU

The Tuatha Dé Danann were a mystical family of people that were said to roam the land for centuries before Christianity made its appearance in the Celtic territories. Translated to mean "children of the Goddess Danu," the Tuatha Dé Danann were said to have perfected the magic arts. The family brought with them four treasures, each wielding incredible powers that made the the Tuatha dé Danann some of the most feared characters in Celtic mythology. The whole race suddenly vanished one day and it's not clear how. Some mythology states that they retreated to fairy caves, and others state they went through a portal to the Otherworld. What is clear is that a massive amount of mythology relied on this family, as it birthed several popular gods and goddesses, such as Boann, Brigid, Dagda, Dian Cécht, Goibniu, Lugh, Nuada, and Macha.

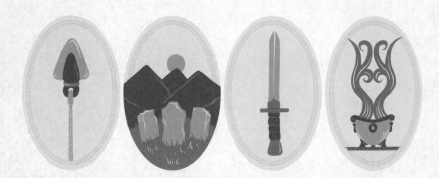

The Four Treasures of Tuatha dé Danann (left to right): The Spear of Lugh, The Stone of Fal, The Sword of Light, and Dagda's Cauldron.

DANU
THE MOTHER GODDESS

The Goddess Danu was considered to be the mother goddess as she was the mother of the Tuatha Dé Danann people. The mythology that surrounds her origins is a little muddy due to the fact that there are many contradictions in the stories about her, and again, nothing was written down. As the goddess of fertility and motherhood, she was also the ruler of wisdom, intellect, and inspiration. The mists of Ireland are said to be her maternal embrace; her earthly symbols are represented below.

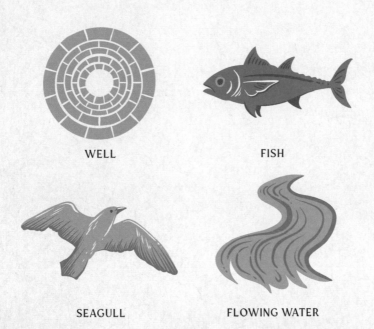

WELL

FISH

SEAGULL

FLOWING WATER

DAGDA
THE GOOD GOD

Dagda is the God of the Earth. Since you know a bit more about Druids now, it might make sense that he was the most highly regarded—and possibly the most important—god on record. With a reverence for the natural world, many mythical stories emerge from the concept of Dagda. He is thought to be the leader of the Tuatha Dé Danann. Dagda had several powerful weapons, including an enormous club that could slay ten men with a single blow with the head, but could also resurrect the dead with the handle. He had a harp that he used to summon the seasons, as well as a cauldron for producing food; it was said that his cauldron had a neverending supply of nourishment. Dagda is an important father figure in Celtic mythology, and he is one of the "good" Celtic gods. He is the father of Aengus, Bodhbh Dearg, Cermait, Midir, and Brigid. He had many lovers, most notably Mórrígan, the Celtic goddess of fate and war.

MÓRRÍGAN
THE GODDESS OF WAR

Known as the "jealous wife" of Dagda, Mórrígan is the Goddess of Fate and War. She is fierce on the battlefield and is the seer of doom and death. In this role, she often appears as a crow that hovers over battles, assigning fates. She encourages warrior courage and valor and strikes fear into the opposition. She is often portrayed as wearing the bloodstained clothing of those fated to perish. She is sometimes referred to in mythology as the Mórrígan, a trio of goddess sisters: Badb, Macha, and Anand—a different iteration of the name Mórrígan.

BRIGID
THE GODDESS
OF FIRE AND HEARTH

The goddess Brigid, also called Brigantia (Celtic for "The High One"), is likely the most famous of Dagda's daughters. Poetry, art, craftwork, prophesy, healing, divination, and fire all fall under the care of Brigid. Due to her affiliation with poetry, she was especially revered by the bards and the filíd, an elite class of Gaelic poets. She was also called simply The Smith, in reference to fire and metalwork. She was said to have mastered (or created) the element of fire and molded the metals of the Underworld through skill and strength, while infusing the weapons with magic. While she might have been the earliest smith god, many more were born into the mythic cannon over time, likely formed from her stories. Saint Brigid is a good example of the Celtic/Christian ideological crossover, along with Saint Patrick and Saint Columba. In the cloisters, the nuns kept a flame burning to represent Brigid's "sacred fire." Each day for nineteen consecutive days, an assigned nun would check on the flame and make sure it was burning brightly, with the twentieth day being tended to by Saint Brigid herself.

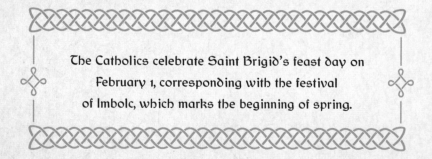

The Catholics celebrate Saint Brigid's feast day on February 1, corresponding with the festival of Imbolc, which marks the beginning of spring.

BRIGID'S PRAYER

May Brigid
bless the house
wherein you dwell,
bless every fireside
every wall, every door,
bless every heart
that beats beneath its roof,
bless every hand that toils to bring it joy,
bless every foot
that walks its portals through.
May Brigid
bless the house
that shelters you.

LUGH
THE GOD OF THUNDERSTORMS

An Irish cultural hero, Lugh was the God of Light. Often, he was referred to as Lugh Lámfada, which translates to mean "of the long hand," since he was known for his prowess with throwing weapons such as long spears. His likeness is frequent in mythology because he was said to lead the Tuatha Dé Danann race to a celebrated victory of the Fomorians during the Battle of Mag Tuired. During this battle, Lugh kills Balor, the one-eyed giant leader of the Fomorians, and also his own grandfather. As difficult as this may have been for Lugh, by doing so he brought on a forty-year period of peace.

AENGUS
THE YOUTHFUL GOD OF LOVE

The son of Dagda, Aengus is a cheerful and youthful god associated with love and summer. Unsurprisingly, he is depicted as a handsome young man in the prime of his physical health.

He famously has the ability to shape-shift, and when he found that the love of his life had been cursed to being a swan forever, Aengus fashioned himself into a swan to be with her. He was also said to turn kisses into birds of flight, his favorite of all the animals.

THE CAILLEACH
THE HAG OF BEIRA

With the power to control the weather and seasons, the Cailleach rules in the winter months between Samhain (November 1) and Beltane (May 1). Thought to have been in partnership with Brigid, it is said that she is handed seasonal responsibility by Brigid as the summer wanes to a close. Due to regional differences, the dates of rulership between the Cailleach can differ according to the seasons.

CERNUNNOS
THE HORNED ONE

Cernunnos was a god typically depicted with horns atop his head, and was closely associated with stags, bulls, and horned serpents. Most likely conceived by the Gauls, he was known as the lord of animals, flora, and fauna, and strongly represents abundance and fertility. Due to his strong pagan associations, he is particularly disturbing to the Roman Christians, who mentioned him in their written records very infrequently due to their disapproval, thus limiting what survives about him today. He is closely related to the Wiccan Horn God.

A PRAYER TO CERNUNNOS

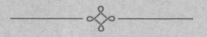

Cernunnos is associated with fertility and vegetation in nature, and is referred to as the Lord of the Forest. With the Druids' central focus on nature as divine, many pray to him or perform rituals in his honor. As the keeper of the trees, and his role as the protector of nature, he can be compared to the Catholic Saint Francis of Assisi, who is often depicted in nature surrounded by animals. It is thought that to pray to Cernunnos is to open the gateway to compassion to the Earth, which, as the supporter of human life, is in turn compassionate to all people.

You don't have to be ancient or a Druid to appreciate this symbolism that speaks of kindness, preservation, appreciation, and compassion. With the hustle of our daily lives taking the wheel most of the time for many of us, it can be difficult to remember to slow down and give gratitude for the life-sustaining beauty of nature and the trees. Praying to Cernunnos is a way to pause and stop taking all of these gifts for granted.

Go into the countryside on a warm day, or find a quiet place in nature, and sit down in a comfortable position. Close your eyes and take several deep, long breaths. Listen to all the sounds around you, from a lightly chirping bird to the wind rustling the leaves of the trees. Allow yourself to fall into a trance and start to feel a connection to the land and to the Earth surrounding you. Ask Cernunnos to come close and give you guidance as to how to help the Earth survive, how to help your loved ones be happy, how to find love, make good friends, and have enough abundance to keep your life pleasurable. Ask him to stand by you forever, giving you protection, guidance, and a healthy dose of common sense whenever this is needed.

GRATITUDE RITUAL

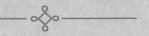

Most people believe that there is a deity or deities that watch over us. Think on your own deity and all you believe they have blessed your life with. Gratitude is important in any practice, so try it here.

1. Write a letter to your deity. Thank them for the specific things in your life that bring you joy. You might list your family, your pets, a reliable job, safe travels, or abundant food.

2. Look in your food storage for an offering of something special. It could be a capful of honey, some dried beans, a little bit of fresh fruit, or a spot of milk.

3. Once you are finished, take a few moments to pray some gratitude while holding your letter close.

4. Go out to an area near your front door or a special place in your yard and bury the letter and the offering. Do not bury anything that can harm the Earth.

5. Now that you've performed this ritual of gratitude, your deity will bless you even more abundantly.

BRIGID'S PROTECTIVE CROSS

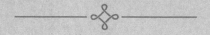

Brigid is the goddess of hearth and fire. Associated with poetry and the arts by the Druids, worshipping Brigid is one of the ways that modern witchcraft and ancient Celtic magic intersect. She is a symbol of the coming of spring, so the best time to perform this ritual is during Imbolc, February 1 through sunset of February 2. It's not necessary to create this on said dates, but if you do, you'll be certain that you're infusing your cross with Brigid's powerful energies.

It is said that Brigid made crosses out of reeds to protect her from evil. In this exercise, you will spark your creativity and make a Brigid's cross to protect your home from negativity. Not everyone has access to natural reeds, so this exercise uses pipe cleaners. You can also use thin, long rolls of paper, natural grasses, flexible strips of wood, or leather. Here, you will need nine pipe cleaners in total.

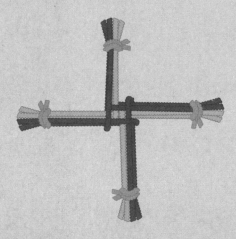

1.

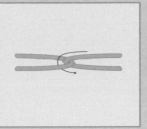

Start with 8 pipe cleaners of the same length (leaving the ninth for later) and fold each of them in half down the center.

2.

Take two of the folded pipe cleaners and loop them together.

3.

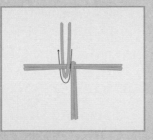

Loop and bend a third pipe cleaner around the center where the previous two were joined at a right angle.

4.

In the opposite direction, loop and bend a fourth pipe cleaner in the center of the main structure at a right angle.

5.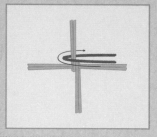

Loop and fold a fifth pipe cleaner around the last one you folded.

6.

Loop and fold a sixth pipe cleaner around the last pipe cleaner you folded as well as the central structure legs that are parallel.

7.

Continue to repeat this step as you go around the structure. Repeat this step until you've used all but the last pipe cleaner (8 out of 9).

8.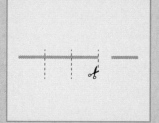

Cut the remaining pipe cleaner into four equal pieces.

9.

Secure the "legs" of the cross by twisting each pipe cleaner piece around each section.

10.

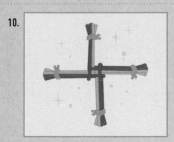

Now that you have your completed cross, you can perform the next magical element: a spell to infuse it with Brigid's energies and blessings.

BLESSING YOUR BRIGID'S CROSS

There are many ways to bless a Brigid's cross, but for our purposes we will conjure the goddess's powers of protection and infuse them into the object. She is one of the most powerful Celtic deities, so be sure to approach this goddess ritual with respect and an open heart. Again, this ritual is best performed during Imbolc, but can be done any time of the year if you feel you need to cleanse your home of negativity. To cleanse the space, you will need a stick of purifying incense and a candle.

Gather:

- ⚜ A stick of incense that has cleansing properties: Rosemary, cinnamon, or sandalwood are all great options. Try to avoid palo santo or white sage. Both palo santo and white sage are at risk of endangerment from over-harvesting native plants. In the spirit of the Druids, kindness to the earth means avoiding any type of harm to the environment.
- ⚜ Sentimental items
- ⚜ Candle

1. Start by setting up an altar on the ledge above your fireplace (if the fireplace is not in use). If the fireplace is in use or you don't have one, you can set up an altar on a flat, clean surface anywhere in your dwelling where it won't be disturbed. To set up an altar, cleanse the space by burning a stick of incense. Then, gather a few items that are sentimental to you, that make you feel safe, and that evoke feelings of self-empowerment and place them on the altar surrounding your candle (far enough away that they won't burn).

2. Take three long, cleansing breaths and clear your mind. Then, visualize your Brigid's cross and your home surrounded by a shield of bright protective light.

3. Invite Brigid into your physical space and light the candle.

4. Sit in quiet contemplation until you feel her power in the room.

5. State your intention out loud. It might look something like, Goddess Brigid, I ask that you protect my home and all who live here from negative energies. Then blow out the candle.

6. Display the cross at your front door, on your hearth, or on your altar.

CHAPTER 8

LORE, GROVES & PORTALS

Celtic mysticism is rife with mystery, magic, and folklore. While the elements that make up the mythology are countless and obscured by a veil of mystery, there are certain specific aspects that have endured through time, invasion, foreign influence, and endangerment. Celtic lore holds many categories and meanings that support the avenues of spirituality, such as groves and portals. As we know, the survival of this magic and lore is owed largely to the Druids, who continue to practice many of the Old Ways, keeping the traditions alive and relevant to modern life.

ANIMAL LORE

The Druids believe that the Earth is sacred, and that includes every little soul that roams it. Just as the trees hold a respected place in the philosophy and worship of the Druids, the female red deer, known as a *hind*, is considered especially sacred. Long ago called "fairy cattle" by the Scots, they believed that they could see the fairies milking the "cows" on the far-away mountaintops. It is said that if you see a hind in nature, or even your dreams, it could mean that good things are coming your way.

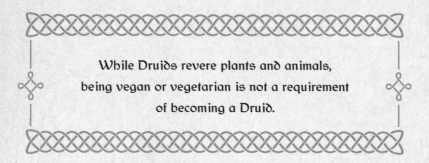

While Druids revere plants and animals,
being vegan or vegetarian is not a requirement
of becoming a Druid.

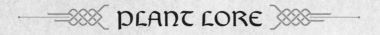

PLANT LORE

Plants are and have been used by Druids in a myriad of ways and have a trove of mythology connected to them.

- ❄ **PLANTS AS FOOD:** The nourishing and life-giving properties of plant-derived food has been relied upon by the Druids for thousands of years, both physically and spiritually. There is a high reverence for the sacred, life-sustaining gifts from the Earth, and much lore is based on them. This natural food is often referred to as *nwyfre*, a Welsh word that roughly translates to mean *sky*. The Druids believe that plants as food connected us with the sky, or the "heavens." The ancient Celts relied on their crops to sustain the kingdoms and people, so many of the most sacred ceremonies are centered around crop season and harvests.

- ❄ **PLANTS IN DRINK:** The Druids have turned plants into magical elixirs and tonics since before they recorded time and involving them in sacred ceremonies is one of the oldest traditions. Druid rituals typically use an elixir called *mead* in their worship. Mead, a mixture of honey, water, and yeast, was associated with community and joy. Elixirs made from mugwort, dandelion, birch, verbena, primrose, and mint, to name a few, were used to connect them with the past, their ancestors, and enhance psychic powers.

⚛ **MEDICINAL PLANTS:** As we've touched on earlier, a major part of plant lore is the use of plants and herbs for healing. There's a long list of medicinal plants, surmised through ancient texts describing plants used holistically, and through mention in popular folklore. One that you might have heard of is valerian root. It was said to be popular at the time for its calming effect, and to this day it can be used to battle anxiety and insomnia. It's not uncommon to find valerian tea at any given grocery store.

⚛ **RITUAL PLANTS:** Flowers and the magic of herbs were and are often used in Druidic celebrations and rituals, especially ceremonies that honor the seasons and the harvest. They can also be pressed into essential oils and used for blessing, anointing, and, in some cases, healing. For Samhain, a celebration of the end of the harvest, altars are loaded with apples, gourds, wheat, and other crops as a show of gratitude for abundance.

Britain was once known as Merlin's Isle due to the abundance of plants and herbs that grow naturally in its climate. Plant lore here can be traced back approximately four thousand years.

When you see a stone circle, the first thing that likely comes to mind is the Druids. While this might be an automatic association, it is speculated that the early ancient Druids used fairy mounds, tree groves, and caves rather than stone circles, and it was the Druids of the last few centuries who started building stone circles. Historians are at odds with the actual use of these, but it is speculated that they were built based on astronomical engineering that helped them to track and predict crop cycles, and that they are therefore sacred. And since they are sacred, they are considered to be magical—and the lore is born.

Modern Druids and other Pagan groups flock to Stonehenge during the summer solstice, which is also known as Litha. This happens when the sun reaches the most northern latitude, which is also known as the tropic of Cancer, and it marks the first day of summer. There are special tours that leave from destinations in London or Bath that people take to Stonehenge to celebrate the summer or winter solstices where they watch the sunrise and the sunset and join in the ceremonies.

Stonehenge, Britain's most famous ancient landmark, was thought to originally be a burial ground and was likely appropriated by the Druids for seasonal ceremonies.

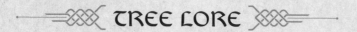

TREE LORE

In the context of the Druids, tree lore hardly needs an introduction. Referred to as the Oak Knowers, the Druids revered trees, the oak in particular, as the most sacred of all. Considered to be full of magic, sacred tree groves are where most of their rituals were held, likely because Druids believed they could boost and revive their own power. The tree offered them spiritual wisdom, and a door to the Otherworld.

THE MAGICAL TREE GROVES

To the Celts, the tree is the powerful link between the person and the Otherworld. The high-reaching branches signified, among other things, humans in the physical world, while the roots beneath the surface were connected to the spiritual world beneath the surface of mortality. As you'll recall, the Gaelic word for oak tree is Dara, which was likely derived from the Greek word *dora*, which means door or gift. This reflects the double meaning that the Druids ascribe to the oak tree: It is the gift of wisdom, and a door to another world. The tree groves of Celtic Ireland were referred to as *nemeton* and were where ceremonies were held for such things as harvests, baby naming, worship, and sacrifice.

Sacred Trees

While the oak is considered to be the most sacred of the Sacred Trees, there are others that the Celts believed to be particularly magical. In fact, they were so revered that raiding tribes or conquering armies were known to cut them down and level the groves as a way to weaken and demoralize the oppressed tribes. These enemies may have recognized sacred groves by Ogham characters carved on the surface of tree trunks. Each letter of the Ogham represents a specific sacred tree, and the alphabetic characters were used to strengthen the power of rituals when carved into stones, grove trees, or wooden staves, also called *runes*.

Sacred Groves for Sacrifice

It can be difficult to fathom how the Druids, whose philosophy supports compassion for all living things, could possibly justify animal and human sacrifice. However, it seems that the practice is rooted in a certain type of kindness, in the sense that these rituals were likely only used during times of great distress of the tribe due to famine or invasion; today we might refer to this as a Hail Mary. It is also speculated that human sacrifice was done in caves or groves, and only on the warriors of their oppressors who were captured in battle. Victims were often drowned as a gift to the god Teutates, who was thought to be the ultimate Protector of the Tribe. Human sacrifices to the god Esus were hung from a tree, and their limbs ripped off. Common iconography usually shows Esus cutting the branches from a tree, lending to the symbolism of the sacrifice ritual. Another god that required human sacrifice was Taranis, the God of Thunder, whose requisite was that the victim be burned alive in a hollow tree. Other methods of sacrifice were impaling, shooting with arrows, or building a large man-shaped tower and filling it with humans and animals before setting it ablaze. Modern Druids shun animal and human sacrifice, but the Druids of old felt deeply that sacrifice helped immeasurably during times of crisis.

Sacred Groves for Divination

One of the most commonly known uses of sacred groves by the Druids is for divination, meaning the forecasting of future events. To achieve these insights, they drew on the observations of clouds, the behavior of birds and other forest wildlife, natural phenomenon, and ancient astrology. The Celts relied on the wren bird as a great prophet and was respectfully referred to as the *druí-en*, the Druid of Birds. They believed there were psychic messages and instructions in the flight paths of the drui-en, their song patterns, and their migrations. Psychic sight could also be enhanced with plant magic, such as eating acorns or wild mint. To read the future of military efforts, they also went to the groves to read the entrails of sacrifice victims to receive messages about battle strategy. A wooden rod made from a yew tree with Ogham characters carved on it was a common tool to predict unlucky days or determine days that are going to be the luckiest of the year.

Sacred Groves as Portals

The sacred groves were also used as portals to different times and places, but most commonly and specifically, the Otherworld. During rituals, it is said that the Druids and seers could access the "door" of the trees, which would reveal to them answers to pressing tribal questions and matters. While portals could also exist in stone circles, caves, mounds of earth, and in burial sites, it was the tree groves that held the most power and wisdom.

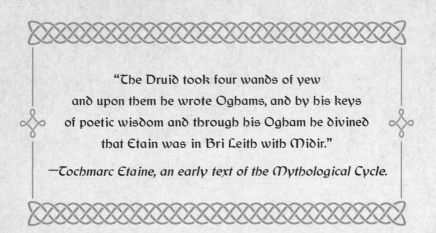

"The Druid took four wands of yew
and upon them he wrote Oghams, and by his keys
of poetic wisdom and through his Ogham he divined
that Etain was in Bri Leith with Midir."

—Tochmarc Etaine, an early text of the Mythological Cycle.

THE TREE OF LIFE

Of particular power, and often planted in the center of a portal grove, was the Crann Bethadh, or Tree of Life. It is planted when a tribe is first geographically settled, and it stands to represent the growth and prosperity of the tribe, and signify the integrity, respect of the Earth, and sanctity of its people. It was here that assembly and ceremonies were held, it provided shelter, and depending on the type of tree, could also provide food and sustenance, although it was typically an oak tree. Riddled with tribal symbolism, the meanings of the crann bethadh varied, but the broad symbolism has much crossover between Celtic subcultures—all under the umbrella of the notion that the tree was a life force for the tribe. Thought to be a portal to the Otherworld and its powers, chieftains were appointed and anointed under the Tree of Life, granting them not only physical strength, but infusing them with ancient wisdom.

Quite possibly the oldest of the Irish symbols, it represents balance and harmony. To the Celts, this meant that it was a representation of the course of one's life. Just as a tree grows, so does one's spiritual wisdom throughout their life, becoming stronger and stronger with age. This is the joining of all the forces of nature in one location (the tree), creating perfect harmony in the universe. Falling asleep under the Tree of Life could result in waking up in the Otherworld, or the realm of the fairies.

In the Celtic oral traditions about this central tree, the significance of the symbol is derived from the ideology that the roots reached into the Underworld, the branches reached for the divine above (the heavens), and the trunk joined the two together on Earth. It also held strong associations of endurance and the integrity of a noble character.

Henry David Thoreau once famously said, "I took a walk in the woods and came out taller than the trees." While to know the true context of this statement we would have to turn to the complete works of Thoreau, it can be assumed that he found a certain magic in being among the trees, and to a Druid, this could begin to sum up the magical gifts that trees can give us. Of course, this doesn't refer to *actually* becoming physically taller, but possibly to a growth in knowledge, wisdom, and understanding of the sacred nature of life. Since the dawn of mankind, trees have been an essential source of life, not just by providing oxygen, sustenance, shelter, and fire, but also as teachers of respect for life, nature, and each other. To be in tune with the lessons they have to give us, we must be open to hearing their messages. This is one of the foundations of Druidry, and, therefore, an overarching foundation of Celtic mysticism.

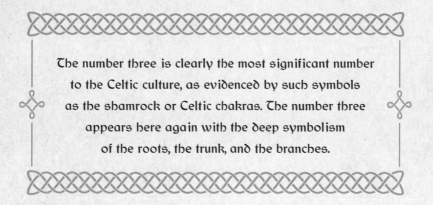

The number three is clearly the most significant number to the Celtic culture, as evidenced by such symbols as the shamrock or Celtic chakras. The number three appears here again with the deep symbolism of the roots, the trunk, and the branches.

A DEEPER LOOK AT TREE MEANINGS

In earlier chapters, we have talked a good amount about not only the power of trees in Celtic mysticism, but also about the way the Druids believed and taught that each tree has magical properties. Much like color magic or herbal magic, tree magic is packed full of symbolism and meaning. The list below shows deeper meanings behind each type of tree that the Celts found to be sacred.

APPLE: Garden, goddess, healing, immortality, love, Underworld.

ASH: Balance, communication, fertility, harmony, healing, knowledge, love divination, prophecy, protection from drowning, transition.

ASPEN: Ancestry, astral planes, eloquence, endurance, healing, money, peace, rebirth, success.

BIRCH: Birth, blessings, creativity, crafting, fertility, goddess, healing, inspiration, love, protection, renewal.

CEDAR: Balance, dreams, healing, immortality, longevity, prosperity, protection, purification, wisdom.

ELM: Birth, compassion, grounding, healing, intuition, love, protection, rebirth, wisdom.

FIR: Birth, far-sightedness, protection, prosperity, rebirth, vitality.

HEMLOCK: Cleansing, mysteries, shadow work.

HOLLY: Courage, death, divinity, healing, luck, protection, rebirth, unity.

MAPLE: Abundance, communication, divination, grounding, love, money, wisdom.

OAK: Ancestry, fertility, health, luck, prosperity, protection, strength, success, wisdom.

PINE: Abundance, emotions, fertility, good luck, healing, immortality, love, prosperity.

SPRUCE: Enlightenment, grounding, healing, intuition, protection, versatility.

WILLOW: Birth, fertility, flexibility, grieving, healing, intuition, knowledge, motherhood.

While all trees are considered sacred by the Celts and Druids, there is a grouping of the most revered referred to as the Sacred Seven: Oak as the most powerful overall, Ash as a prophet with maternal leanings, Apple as a symbol of fertility, both in women and the crops that supported the tribes, Hazel that sparks wisdom and inspiration, Alder as a symbol of rebirth, Elder as rest, quietude, and reflection, and the Yew, symbolizing death and resurrection.

The Celtic belief that trees communicated with each other is not as far fetched as it might seem. Through what scientists call a mycorrhizal network, the roots of trees that are near each other can communicate and also help each other in times of stress. For instance, in hot weather, a tree may become too dry so it will ask a nearby tree for help, whereupon the second tree will tap into the roots of the first and feed it a little water to keep it going. The same goes for a tree that becomes short of a particular nutrient. A nearby tree will reach out its roots and feed the necessary nutrient to the hungry tree.

COMMUNICATING WITH TREES

When connecting to a tree, always approach the tree with respect and ask if you can sit and commune with it. A communication from the tree might come in the form of an inner stirring, a gentle breeze, a rustling of leaves, a shadow cast, or a sense of the deep ancient wisdom that it holds. If you have a sense that you are blocked, spiritually or mentally, listen to that communication as well. This might not be the tree that you're being called to commune with, so respect the message and move on until you find a sense of where and which tree you are invited to be in communion with.

It can be tricky to communicate with trees because it relies heavily on your intuition. One way to get the most of these sessions is to just sit comfortably, close your eyes, and listen. Messages and insights will come through. When you feel you've received what the tree offers you, thank the tree by placing your hand gently on the trunk and either saying *thank you*, or by reciting your own prayer of gratitude. Come back frequently to commune and strengthen the bond between you and the tree.

Messenger Trees

Sometimes when you enter a forest you may come across what we call "talking trees." These are trees with branches or trunks that rub up against other trees, and when the wind blows you can hear them creaking. These are the *messenger trees*; they are communicating audibly so that others can hear what they have to say. Start by finding one of these trees if you can, as they are the speakers of the forests. Listen to their creaking, sit at the base of the trunk and let the creaking reverberate through your body. Put your ear to the trunk and hear the creaking throughout the tree. Play with different ways to hear the sounds and pay close attention to the messages that your intuition is picking up.

The Voice of the Wind

Another way to hear a tree's message is to listen to the wind and the way that it blows through the leaves, needles, and branches. Place your ear to the bark and listen to the wind blowing through the tree. Gaze upward through the branches and observe the wind influencing the motion of the branches and leaves. What you hear will be based on the tree itself, as the different wood density between tree types creates different reverberations. Tree echoes have their own kind of music depending on the tree and the weather. The message relies on what the tree wants you to know.

WINTER TREES

The easiest way to observe a tree communication is to watch the patterns of light and color cast by the leaves and branches play out on the forest floor; a dance inspired by the season and the climate of the day or night. In the fall, you can walk through the forest and discover the most beautiful patchwork patterns of fallen leaves and colors. All these things have messages to share for those looking and listening. Pay attention to the time of the year, because some tree species are most active and engaged in the late winter, early spring, or when they are in full foliage, but as winter approaches, all trees, even the conifers, slow down a bit.

You can't do much to commune with trees in winter because they are at rest, making it a good time to honor them as they prepare for rebirth in the spring. When dormant, their messages are likely to be focused on rest, rejuvenation, inner peace, calm, and your own healing prior to a spiritual rebirth.

USE YOUR SENSES

An important aspect of communing with the trees is using your five senses: get close to the tree and see how it smells; look closely at each part of the tree and notice what makes it unique and special; if it is a fruit tree (and you're familiar enough to know the fruit is safely edible), taste its fruit; listen to the sounds that it makes, its leaves make, the branches make; run your hand down the trunk and palm its leaves while appreciating the textures. Also observe the tree in differing situations: Stand with a tree while it is raining and watch how the water runs down the trunk, gets into the cracks, creates little bubbles that soften and soak bits of moss growing in the trunk; look at the tree in moonlight, in sunlight, or in the fog. Observe the branches and leaves close up and from a distance. Notice the patterns that the branches grow out in, how thick they are, and how twisted or straight. Look for any effect the landscape has on the tree and its root systems. You can learn so very much by visiting the tree every day for a year, observing it in all its seasons and in all weathers. Like a friend, you must commit the time to get to know it.

As climate change continues to become an increasingly pressing issue, modern science and ancient Celtic mysticism intersect in increasingly visible ways. Diana Beresford-Kroeger, a botanist and biochemist with Celtic roots, has been applying the Druidic concept of the sacred nature of trees to modern scientific problems, and her voice is finally being heard. According to her, if everyone on earth planted six native trees over the course of six years, we could solve the climate change problem. On her own property, she cultivates trees, plants, and herbs that are considered sacred in the Celtic mystic traditions and employs Druidic philosophy through the study of the medicinal, scientific, and spiritual aspects of each plant.

PROTECTION OIL
OF ANCESTORS

This enchanted oil is infused with the energy of your ancestors and can be applied any day, at any time, to call on and reinforce their protective energies. As the ovates once did, this spell uses herbs and essential oils that not only bring protection, but also heal. Apply the oil wherever you need an added boost of protection: dab the dashboard of your car, dab it on your wrist when you're walking into a precarious situation or before you have to meet with someone whose energy brings you down, dab it on the heads of the children before they leave the house, or dab it at the top of each door and window in your house to protect your home from negative forces. The options are endless! Gather the following items:

- White candle for protection, one brown candle for nature
- 6 whole cloves to banish hostile forces
- 1 bay leaf for protection
- 3 drops ylang-ylang essential oil to banish anxiety and fear
- 3 drops tea tree oil as a nod to the ovates
- 3 drops bergamot oil for protection
- A clean container or jar with a lid
- A carrier oil such as olive or coconut oil (must be skin-safe)

1.   Begin by setting up an altar. If you don't have one established, you can simply find a clean table-top space that is not cluttered or crowded. Place your candles on your altar on a heat-safe surface, along with the cloves, bay leaf, and oils.

2.   Fill your jar about two-thirds full with your carrier oil, and place it back on your altar.

3.   On the bay leaf, write down what you'd like to ask your ancestors for protection from. If it's a more general request, you can write something like, "Spiritual negativity."

4.   Light both the white and brown candles.

5.   In your oil jar, add the bay leaf, the whole cloves, and the essential oils. Secure the lid and gently rock the jar back and forth to blend the elements. As you do, recite: I call on you, my ancestors, my guides, my faithful protectors. Infuse this oil now with your energy and shield. Protect me always.

6.   Place your oil jar under the light of the candles and allow them to burn for one hour before blowing them out. When you blow out the candles, chant the spell again.

CONCLUSION

Ancient Celtic wisdom translates easily into a modern mindset and it's my hope that this book will compel you to continue to explore the abundance the Celtic culture has to offer and dig deeper into their histories, myths, lore, and magic. I hope you feel inspired to learn more about the environment in which you dwell; what plants and trees, herbs and flowers grow around you, and how you can harness the magic they have to share. I encourage you to honor the spirits of the land by treating the Earth respectfully and kindly. Embody these ancient people by taking awe at the majesty and secret messages of the trees, forage for natural materials for spells, crafts, and recipes, acknowledge the ancestors before you, and become connected with the deep, ancient wisdom of our Earth.

This is an exciting journey, but it is also one of personal responsibility. Celtic magic is a powerful and ancient force and should be approached with respect and an open heart. I encourage you to continue to be curious, ask questions, and explore this mysterious arena. This book is a mere introduction and there is so much more to learn. Thank you for taking this journey with me. Go forth and be abundant in spirit, in wisdom, and in magic.

AN OLD IRISH BLESSING

May the road rise to meet you,
May the wind be always at your back,
May the sun shine warm upon your face,
And the rain fall soft upon your fields,
And until we meet again,
May God hold you in the palm of his hand.

INDEX

First published in 2023 by Wellfleet, an imprint of The Quarto Group,
142 West 36th Street, 4th Floor, New York, NY 10018, USA
T (212) 779-4972 F (212) 779-6058 www.Quarto.com

Wellfleet titles are also available at discount for retail, wholesale, promotional, and bulk purchase. For details, contact the Special Sales Manager by email at specialsales@quarto.com or by mail at The Quarto Group, Attn: Special Sales Manager, 100 Cummings Center Suite 265D, Beverly, MA 01915 USA.

10 9 8 7 6 5 4 3 2

ISBN: 978-1-57715-346-7

Library of Congress Control Number: 2022948207

Publisher: Rage Kindelsperger
Creative Director: Laura Drew
Managing Editor: Cara Donaldson
Editor: Sara Bonacum
Cover and Interior Design: Amelia LeBarron

Printed in China

This book provides general information on various widely known and widely accepted images that tend to evoke feelings of strength and confidence. However, it should not be relied upon as recommending or promoting any specific diagnosis or method of treatment for a particular condition, and it is not intended as a substitute for medical advice or for direct diagnosis and treatment of a medical condition by a qualified physician. Readers who have questions about a particular condition, possible treatments for that condition, or possible reactions from the condition or its treatment should consult a physician or other qualified healthcare professional.

The Quarto Group denounces any and all forms of hate, discrimination, and oppression and does notcondone the use of its products in any practices aimed at harming or demeaning any group or individual.